Forest Finance Simplified

Seventh Edition

Brooks C. Mendell, Ph.D.
Forisk Consulting

Forisk Press
Athens, Georgia

Published by Forisk Press

For information about this book, contact:
    Forisk Consulting
    PO Box 5070
    Athens, GA 30604
    770.725.8447

Cover image by Getty Images

ISBN 978-0-9896150-4-4

Table of Contents

About this Book

"Life is made up of a series of judgments on insufficient data, and if we waited to run down all our doubts, it would flow past us." – Learned Hand

The improper or selective use of financial metrics can distort results and mislead investment decisions. This book distills finance themes into a question-and-answer format and series of brief observations for those who want an accessible reference and introduction to analyzing investment opportunities. This includes anyone who needs to understand the identification, valuation, and ranking of investments, especially as they relate to forestry and natural resources. It also serves those who want to refresh their finance toolkit and think broadly about capital budgeting and the "market for money."

This handbook succinctly helps readers:

- Identify and communicate key financial issues for a given investment, with applications in forestry and timberland.
- Differentiate and explain the pros and cons of traditional approaches to financial analysis.
- Analyze, rank, and benchmark the value and performance of forest management activities and timberland investments.
- Avoid common errors associated with investment decisions.

Readers are assumed to have a basic knowledge of accounting, finance, calculators, and spreadsheets (e.g. Excel).

This book would not be possible without the support and editorial suggestions from friends and colleagues at Forisk – especially Heather Clark, Amanda Lang, Pamela Smith, David Rossi, and Shawn Baker – and the questions and feedback from the thousands of students who have participated in our *Applied Forest Finance* workshops and seminars over the years. Thank you!

The freedom and opportunity to write books, teach courses, and grow a forestry research business depends on the love and support of my wife, Liz, and daughters, Dani and Ellery. For this, for them, and for many other things, I am forever grateful.

Introduction: What is Finance? What is Forest Finance?

Answer:
Finance refers to the management and analysis of capital from all sources, from cash to debt to equity, and investments. Forest finance is the language and analysis of managing forest resources as investments.

Discussion:
   What is a tree worth? For investors and businesses, the value of a tree is determined by the returns on the capital committed to owning, growing, and marketing the tree. In forestry, financial analysis supports decisions such as the optimal rotation, intermediate harvests and silvicultural strategies, and the buying and selling of timberlands.
   Basic financial tools and frameworks help organize our thinking to make optimal decisions given what we know at the time. As forestry pioneer and educator Carl Schenck wrote years ago:

   "No capitalist and no forester is forced to adopt a financial formula or equation when determining the merits of an investment. The equation merely illustrates a logical manner of financial thinking…."

   Forest finance and financial analysis provide forest owners and investors with methods for selecting the best option given their objectives. It addresses the question, "What approaches can we use to screen, value, and rank potential forestry investments?"

Finance Addresses Three Sets of Questions
   The fundamental economic value of an asset derives from the cash flows generated by the asset. The price of an asset can vary from this fundamental value over time because of uncertainty associated with future cash flows and investment alternatives. From this context, the application of finance in forestry addresses three sets of questions.
   First, how do we identify, screen, and value investment opportunities? In forestry, these include timberland acquisitions and

forest management decisions. This set of questions deals with the **"investment decision"** and accounts for our opportunity costs.

Second, how do we pay for this investment? This addresses the **"financing decision"**, including the use of leverage and the suitable deployment of available capital for investment.

Third, how and when is the appropriate time to divest – to sell – the property, or to sell timber to maximize profits? We refer to this set of questions as the **"exit decision."**

While forestry investments require capital, capital is a limited resource. We apply financial tools to identify, evaluate, and track these investments. In short, finance as a discipline, with forest finance as an application, describes a method of investment decision-making.

Finance in One Formula

For me, one basic formula summarizes all investment analysis:

$$\textbf{Value} \quad = \quad \frac{\textbf{Cash Flows}}{(1 + \textbf{Discount Rate})^{\text{Time}}}$$

This formula frames the "big picture" as it relates to questions of finance and investment strategy. It contains four key parts: value (or measure); cash flows; time (and timing), and discount rate. As an equation, you need to know three pieces to calculate the fourth. In this case, certain elements are extremely "knowable" while others must be estimated or given (e.g., the discount rate).

In ten minutes and with a few questions based on this framework, we can assess the ability and competitiveness of any investor seeking to buy or sell timberland in each business environment. The four elements represent levers over which different investors have varying levels of flexibility.

- Value references the primary objective, usually financial, of the investor. It asks, "what are we trying to answer? What are the appropriate criteria?" These usually include, at a minimum, net present value (NPV) and internal rate of return (IRR).
- Cash flows refer to all expected sources of costs and revenues. It asks, "how well can we estimate expected cash flows?" This means developing points of view on future wood flows (i.e. growth and

yield modeling), stumpage prices (i.e. forecasting), and expenses (i.e. silviculture activities and taxes).

- <u>Discount rate</u> refers to risk and asks, "what is the appropriate hurdle rate or expected return for this asset and opportunity?"
- <u>Time</u> can refer to the length of the expected investment – "what is the investment period?" – or the timing – "when?" – of a potential investment decision.

In assessing an investor's situation, we ask, "how many of these levers can you pull?" A corporation may have zero flexibility with the discount rate because they have a hurdle rate mandated by the Board of Directors. An institutional investor may have some flexibility with the discount rate, but little room to adjust timing, as they need a project of exactly 10 or 20 years. Differences across objectives, such as cash flows versus value preservation, affect the competitiveness of different investors looking at the same timberland properties.

For a range of objectives, finance represents a tradeoff between today and tomorrow. To paraphrase forest economist David Wear of the U.S. Forest Service, **an investment is the dedication of today's resources to tomorrow's production**. Investing in something now – a factory, research, or timberland – means giving something today to gain in the future. The tools of finance help us evaluate the tradeoffs and assess whether each opportunity meets our objectives.

Forest Finance Builds on Two Core Economic Concepts

Financial analysis depends on two economic concepts from utility theory. One, **we prefer more money rather than less**. Two, **we prefer dollars today rather than dollars tomorrow**. These principles hold for everyone from kindergarteners to investment bankers; they help explain all basic financial criteria related to investing.

First, utility describes our behavior in terms of how we attempt to increase or decrease our "relative" satisfaction. Utility theory is used for everything from predicting the success of pornography and shopping on the Internet to how much sugar people put in their coffee. Utility theory tells us that, from an economic standpoint, bigger is better; give us Park Avenue over Skid Row. Supersize me.

Second, utility theory speaks to our preference for consuming goods now rather than waiting until later. This gets to the time value of money. A dollar today is worth more than a dollar in the future; if you have it now, you have choices and can do something with it today. We prefer consuming to saving.

In forest finance, these concepts encourage us to **maximize net present value (bigger is better)** and **invest in forest management that shortens rotations (time value of money).** They remind us to **always consider the opportunity cost** of putting capital into forests versus our next best investment alternative. These principles guide our use of discounted cash flow (DCF) models and related investment criteria.

Four Categories of Forest Investment Questions

Most decisions in forest finance build on these economic concepts. However, my experience is that investment errors are less about misunderstanding economic theories and more associated with asking poorly defined questions, making unsupported assumptions, and missing simple spreadsheet errors. While we cannot control the state of the economy, there remain things we can control when allocating capital, starting with how we define the key issue or question.

In forestry, we can organize fundamental investment questions into four categories:

Category of Questions	Forestry Examples
1. Accept/Reject: Does this project or investment satisfy our rate of return or opportunity cost expectations?	• Timberland acquisitions • Buy different type of seedlings • Mid-rotation fertilization
2. Rank/Prioritize: Of the qualifying projects or investments, which should we choose or consider further?	• Choosing between properties • Choosing silviculture options • Deciding where to fertilize (first)
3. Value/Valuation: What is this asset worth?	• Deciding what to pay • Deciding on sale (or "no sale") price
4. Optimize: How do we maximize the value of the asset we own?	• Optimal rotation age • Optimal forest management strategy

When deciding where to allocate limited capital, we benefit by systematically applying criteria for identifying, ranking, and optimizing the available options. Choosing which criterion to use, which we review in the following chapters, depends on the question we're asking.

SIDEBAR: When is a Forest Mature?

Forest economists distinguish between "biological" and "economic" maturity. "Maturity" references rotation ages that maximize sustainable harvest volumes or sustainable economic returns.

The optimum biological rotation uses the mean annual increment (MAI), which is the average forest growth per acre per year. We calculate MAI by dividing total forest volume by its age. The maximum MAI is the maximum sustained yield (MSY), which reflects the most timber that can be harvested sustainably without reducing the forest inventory. The age of MSY is called the optimal biological rotation.

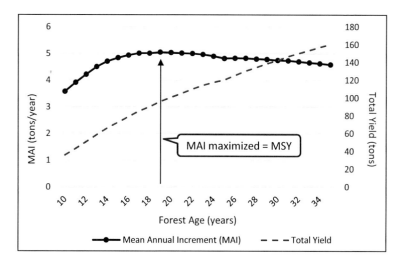

The optimum economic rotation addresses financial maturity. Forests are financially mature when their annual growth rate in value equals the target rate of return or cost of capital. This rotation age is usually shorter than the biologically optimal rotation age.

In sum, maximizing MAI is the best criterion if your time value of money is zero. MAI considers biological growth, not your financial opportunity cost.

How Does Forest Growth Relate to Opportunity Cost?

As trees age, their growth rate declines. As growth declines, financial appreciation slows, and annual returns ultimately decrease. Trees adding the same volume of wood each year represents a small annual return, just as cash yield falls as a percentage when the value of an asset increases.

Consider how a $1 gain on $10 is 10% growth while a $1 gain on $100 is a 1% increase. Forests exhibit a similar dynamic as they approach maturity. Eventually, returns from tree growth fall below the opportunity cost, indicating a mature forest.

With no opportunity costs, a landowner should harvest trees when the annual increment of forest growth crosses MAI, which maximizes the biological output of the forest. With no opportunity cost, the financially optimal rotation age equals the biologic optimum.[1]

Finance Supports the Allocation of Resources

Let's clarify the organizing principles. First, timberlands and mills and other investments require capital. Second, investors have the capital. Third, investors have opportunity costs. If long-term U.S. Treasuries offered a 7% yield, net returns from alternate investments should exceed this. **The cash flows and expected gains spinning off an asset justify the capital allocated to that asset**.

In forestry, the ability to get more production from fewer acres helps us move resources to when and where they can be more productive. While Mark Twain said, "Buy land, they're not making it anymore," innovators and researchers spent decades working around this Earthly constraint. Consider fertilizers and improved seedlings. Consider office towers, sewage treatment plants, and crematoriums. Each helps us do more on fewer acres or take advantage of neglected acres more productively.

This is analogous to the roles played by markets for financial investments. Capital markets, like those for stocks and bonds, bring savers and borrows together, moving financial resources across space and time to where they are needed most. This is also the case in forestry.

---

[1] This holds when the forest has a single product (and single price). With multiple forest products and price points, this can differ.

Primary Financial Criteria and Tools: NPV, IRR, and BLV

Financial analysis helps investors rank investment options, evaluate investment risk, and assess the impact of each investment or project on the overall portfolio or firm. **This section emphasizes the proper application of financial criteria to help investors and managers identify, value, and rank forest investment alternatives.**

In addition to addressing common queries from students and investors, this section answers topical questions such as:

- How and when do we use net present value (NPV)?
- How and when do we use internal rate of return (IRR)?
- How and when do we use bare land value (BLV)?

How Are Financial Decisions Made in Forestry?

Answer:

Present value provides the most appropriate basis for comparing the profitability of potential forestry investments over time. With unlimited capital, project selection is easy: invest in all projects with a positive net present value. But who has unlimited capital?

Discussion:

Present value (PV), the value today of cash flows generated in the future, is the most reliable of all investment criteria. Why? Because our general orientation in forest finance and economics is to maximize wealth rather than maximize profits. While these objectives usually coincide for long-term investments, they sometimes conflict over short timeframes.

For example, firms may increase timber harvesting or reduce spending on fertilizer or weed control to satisfy quarterly profit or cash flow needs. While helpful to near-term financial goals, these decisions may reduce long-term forest productivity and, ultimately, firm wealth.

Timber management requires an appreciation of the **time value of money** since costs may exceed revenues in all years until we start harvesting trees. As benefits received in the future have less value than the same benefits received today, **we adjust cash flows to a common point in time when evaluating investments.**

12

Discounted cash flow (DCF) techniques provide the most common basis for addressing operational, investment, and capital budgeting decisions facing timber managers. DCF criteria include, for example, **net present value** (NPV) and **internal rate of return** (IRR).

As investment criterion, DCF techniques give proper "accept-reject" signals by satisfying two key financial principles. One, **bigger is better**. We want to maximize our wealth and returns from each investment. Two, **now is better**. We also want to generate these returns as soon as possible.

Compounding and Discounting

The concept of the **time value of money** teaches us that a dollar today is worth more than a dollar in the future. The calculations for how the value of money changes over time rely on the math of compounding and discounting.

Cash flows can be adjusted to the beginning of the investment (discounted), end of the investment life (compounded), or some intermediate point. We discount (or compound) at the "cost of capital", which is the minimum required return for the investment. This **discount rate** – also known as the hurdle rate or alternative rate of return – is not directly observable. We cannot look it up in a "Discount Rate Bible"; it must be estimated or selected.

In forestry and natural resources, many questions involve compounding, from those related to financial returns to others on population and biological growth rates. Compounding applies rates of change to the value of assets, volume of tree growth, or population of insects as it changes, not just to the starting amount.

We illustrate the financial impact of compounding by comparing it to linear (simple) growth. Assume we invest $100 at 10% for 20 years. After one year, our investment grows to $110, adding $10 (10% of $100). If this growth continued linearly, it would add another $10 each year for 19 more years. After 20 years, the value of our investment would be $300.

Alternately, with compound interest, we earn on the interest payments themselves, as well. After one year, our investment also grows to $110. After two years, it grows to $121, adding $11 (10% of $110), and to $133 after three and finally, after twenty years, reaches $673 (figure) after growing at a compounding rate of 1.10 per annum.

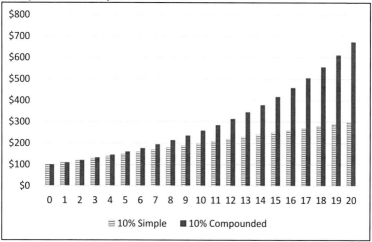

Compound vs Simple Interest: $100 Invested 20 Years at 10%

Legend: ▦ 10% Simple ▪ 10% Compounded

In short, compound interest grows exponentially; simple interest grows linearly. Money moves up and down a timeline through compounding (into the future) and discounting (back to today from the future).

The basic formula for estimating future value clarifies this. First, consider the simple growth of an investment during its first year:

> *Future Value* = *Present Value * (1 + rate)*
> = *growth of our initial investment for one year*

From our example, this means the future value is a function of our initial $100 growing 10% for one year, or $110 = $100 * (1.10).

Next, consider the compound growth of an investment made for multiple years, or *n* years.

> *Future Value* = *Present Value * (1 + rate)^n*
> = *growth of our investment for "n" years*

From our example, the initial $100 investment growing for 20 years at a compounded 10% produces a future value of $673, or $673 = $100 * (1.10)^{20}.

If we turn this around and ask, "what is the present value of $673 received 20 years in the future assuming a 10% discount rate?", the formula would be:

Present Value   = Future Value/(1 + rate)^n

This gives us the discounted value in today's dollars of an investment received *n* years in the future. Our future value of $673 discounted for 20 years at 10% per year produces a present value of $100, or $100 = $673/(1.10)^{20}.

Compounding and discounting provide the analytic means to quantify the time value of money. Through applying a discount rate (opportunity cost), compounding quantifies the future value of investments made today, while discounting calculates the value today of expected future cash flows. In mirroring how compounding grows value, discounting "erodes" or diminishes the future value at a compounding rate.

Compounding is a powerful concept. It informs the advice to children and those just starting their careers to start saving and investing early: crank the flywheel of compounding interest and let it go to work for you as soon as possible!

However, future value is not the primary metric used to make investment decisions in forestry, or generally.

How and When Do We Use NPV?

Answer:

Net present value (NPV) compares the value of cash flows received in the future with the capital required for an investment today. The decision rule is to accept projects with NPVs greater than or equal to zero.

Discussion and Example:

Net present value (NPV) "nets" the present value of future cash flows against the initial investment made today given a pre-determined discount rate or expected rate or return.

$$NPV \ = \ - \text{ Initial Investment} + \frac{\text{Cash Flows}_{Year}}{(1 + \text{Discount Rate})^{Year}}$$

Consider a simple timber management example. Assume we establish a forest today by investing $250 per acre in site preparation, seedlings, and planting. Assume this forest grows and generates $350 per acre from a thinning at age 17 and $1,800 per acre from a final harvest (clear cut) at age 26. Assume a discount rate of 6% real (does not include inflation).

Initial Investment	-$250
Discount Rate	6%

Year	Cash Flow	Present Value	Notes
0	-$250	-$250	Site prep and plant
17	$350	$130	Thinning
26	$1,800	$396	Final harvest
NPV		$276	

The project generates a positive NPV of $276 per acre. What does this mean? First, since the NPV is positive, we earned at least 6% annually on our initial investment of $250. Second, we earned an additional $276 in present value. In sum, we exceeded our expected rate of return and, assuming solid estimates of future cash flows, created additional wealth for the firm or ourselves.

NPV generally takes the investor's point of view. We look to the future. (As a former microeconomics professor told me, "Look right!") Previous investments in the forest are irrelevant; they represent sunk costs. Focus on the forest's ability to generate returns in the future given its current condition and our view of markets.[2] The decision rule tells us that selecting NPV positive projects increases firm value.

DISCUSSION: Should a Negative NPV Automatically Kill a Potential Investment?

Short answer:
No. Let's discuss.

Discussion:
Net present value (NPV) is the present value of future revenues minus the present value of all costs. It is a measure of wealth creation

---

[2] As one timberland owner told me, "Investing in timberland and planting trees are acts of faith.... You decide whether or not society will be using wood and forest products in 30 years. Ask yourself, 'Will there be markets for wood products?'"

relative to the discount rate. A negative or zero NPV does not indicate "no value." Rather, a zero NPV means that the investment earns a rate of return equal to the discount rate. If you discount cash flows using a 6% real rate and produce a $0 NPV, then the analysis indicates your investment would earn a 6% real rate of return.

A negative NPV means that the present value of the costs exceeds the present value of the revenues at the assumed discount rate. Most investments produce a negative NPV if the discount rate is high enough. Therefore, it makes sense to double-check the estimated costs, look for ways to economize, review the revenue sources to seek potential enhancements, and revisit the assumed discount rate.

A pension fund consultant once asked me, "does it make sense to use discount rates for timberland investments that are below the expected returns for the total investment?"

My response was, "well, isn't that the point?" We create value by identifying investments where the returns exceed the risk-adjusted discount rate. If the discount rate and rate of return are equal, we have a zero NPV opportunity on our hands.

Consider the use of NPV "philosophically." There <u>will be random error</u> in forest growth models and estimates of future cash flows, so a marginal project will give a positive NPV result 50% of the time. In a competitive marketplace, most projects "should" have zero NPVs in the long run, as high NPV opportunities attract competition from new investors and drive down expected returns. In the end, any positive NPV project should have a "story" supported by the data.

Advantages and Disadvantages of Using NPV

What are key advantages and disadvantages associated with using NPV as an investment and capital budgeting criterion? <u>Advantages include</u>:

- NPV provides an unambiguous measure. It estimates wealth creation from the potential investment in today's dollars, given the applied discount rate.
- NPV accounts for investment size.
- NPV is straightforward to calculate.
- NPV uses cash flows rather than net earnings (which includes non-cash items such as depreciation).

- NPV recognizes the time value of money (unlike cash-on-cash returns or simple payback period). For forestry investments, which tend to be long-term, this is critically and entirely appropriate.
- NPVs are additive. If you have multiple projects and excess capital, you can add up projects to get a sense of aggregate wealth creation from all investable projects.

Disadvantages include:
- A discount rate must be selected. NPV also assumes the discount rate is constant over the life of the investment or project. Discount rates, like interest rates, can and do change year-to-year. Consider capitalization ("cap") rates in commercial real estate. Benchmarks move. Opportunity costs change.
- NPV assumes you can accurately assess and predict future cash flows. While your crystal ball may prove infallible, mine shows cracks at times.
- For some, it is an intuitively difficult concept to grasp.

How and When Do We Use IRR?

Answer:
   Internal rate of return (IRR) is the discount rate that makes NPV equal to zero; it reflects the compounded return produced by a project. IRR is best used in tandem with other measures, especially in forestry. Why? IRR can mislead if we fail to account for the reinvestment assumptions for intermediate cash flows. The decision rule is to accept projects with IRRs greater than or equal to the cost of capital.

Discussion and Example:
   As the discount rate that makes discounted revenues equal to discounted costs, IRR makes NPV equal to zero. IRR is the _result_ of a calculation; it is not a pre-determined hurdle rate or discount rate. The math behind IRR acts like a search-and-destroy mission in pursuit of the rate (or rates) that produces no excess returns or losses. **IRR is a heat-seeking missile for the zero NPV solution**.

Forestry professionals like IRR because it is easily understood and compared with returns from other investments or projects. With a single initial investment and a single future cash return (such as planting trees today and harvesting them in N years), estimating IRR is straightforward:

$$\textbf{IRR} \ = \ \left[\frac{\textbf{Cash Revenue}}{\textbf{Cash Investment}} \right]^{\textbf{1/N}} \textbf{- 1}$$

Assume we spend $250 today (year 0) to harvest $2,000 worth of trees in 25 years. Using the IRR formula, this gives us:

$(2{,}000/250)^{(1/25)} - 1 = 8.7\%.$

If our discount rate or cost of capital is below the IRR of 8.7%, then **we should invest** based on this result.

In practice, investors and analysts use NPV and IRR together to offer a complete view of potential investments. While IRR clarifies how an investment accumulates returns, NPV estimates the gains (or losses) in actual wealth.

Understand IRR's Reinvestment Rate Assumption

IRR does not, per se, provide a "proper" signal for the risk of an investment. Rather, IRR, by definition, provides the rate of return that produces an NPV of zero <u>given the assumed cash flows</u>.

IRR has limitations. It can give unrealistic rates of return because of the reinvestment rate assumption. **IRR assumes that all intermediate cash flows are reinvested at the IRR.**

What does this mean? Why is this problematic? IRR measures how fast profits accumulate in an investment. This depends on the assumed rate of return generated by investing intermediate revenues that occur prior to the end of the investment. Since IRR assumes that the rate of return estimated for the entire investment – the IRR itself – applies to intermediate cash flows for "reinvestment," the results can be misleading. Therefore, we use IRR cautiously.

If we estimate a 20% IRR for a 10-year project that generates cash flows each year, the math indicates that to get the 20% return, each cash flow must be reinvested at 20% annually until the project matures. Is this realistic? Can we take all cash flows generated by a given project and immediately reinvest them into the same project and earn the same rate of return on this reinvested cash?

When the estimated IRR exceeds the true reinvestment rate, it overestimates the actual IRR of the project. NPV, on the other hand, assumes that interim cash flows are reinvested at the discount rate. **IRR provides a true indication of annual investment returns only when the project generates no interim cash flows**, or when interim cash flows can be invested at the actual IRR, which is uncommon.

How can we account for the reinvestment rate issue (other than avoiding the use of IRR)? One approach uses a **modified internal rate of return** (MIRR) that assumes interim cash flows are reinvested at the firm's cost of capital or some other reinvestment rate.

How Do We Use Modified Internal Rate of Return (MIRR)?

How do we calculate MIRR? First, find the present value of negative cash flows (costs) using the discount rate or cost of capital. Next, we calculate the future value of positive cash flows using the assumed reinvestment rate for these cash flows. **The final math provides the rate that equates the future value of the positive cash flows to the present value of the negative cash flows**.

Often, MIRR is less than the estimated IRR (which can make project sponsors unhappy). Here's an example using the MIRR formula (which is also a standard spreadsheet function):

$$\text{MIRR} = \sqrt[n]{\frac{Future\ Value(positive\ cash\ flows, reinvestment\ rate)}{-Present\ Value(negative\ cash\ flows, discount\ rate)}} - 1$$

Where n = Number of periods (years) for each cash flow
Future Value = Calculated to end of final period
Present Value = Calculated to beginning of first period

Consider a four-year investment with the following cash flows and assumptions. We specify a discount rate of 6% (which reflects our cost of capital) and a reinvestment rate of 8% (which represents another project where we put cash generated by this investment). Using normal DCF criteria, the project looks attractive with an NPV of $944 and an IRR of 26% (which far exceeds our 6% discount rate).

Rate	
Reinvestment	8%
Discount	6%

Year	Cash Flow	Present Value	Future Value
0	-$1,000	-$1,000	
1	-$500	-$472	
2	$500		$583
3	$1,000		$1,080
4	$1,500		$1,500
NPV	$944		
IRR	26%		
Totals		-$1,472	$3,163

For MIRR, we calculate the present value of the negative cash flows using the discount rate (-$1,472) and the future value of the positive cash flows using the reinvestment rate ($500*(1+8%)^2 + $1,000*(1+8%)^1 + $1,500 = $3,163).

Then, we use the MIRR formula:

$$\text{MIRR} = \sqrt[4]{\frac{\$3,163}{\$1,472}} - 1 = \left(\frac{\$3,163}{\$1,472}\right)^{\frac{1}{4}} - 1 = 21\%$$

The MIRR of 21% differs from the estimated IRR of 26%. The gap reflects the difference between reinvesting the cash from years 2 and 3 at the reinvestment rate of 8% versus the estimated IRR of 26%. **As analysts, we provide a cleaner, more transparent assessment of investment potential by specifying a reinvestment rate.**

What are Key Considerations for Using MIRR?

Modified internal rate of return (MIRR) requires you or your analyst to specify a reinvestment rate. It forces a decision that better complements NPV and provides superior guidance for investment decisions.

A conservative approach parks intermediate cash flows into a savings account or bond until the end of the investment period. Or you may have projects "in the queue" which will use cash flows generated along the way. With MIRR, you can test its sensitivity with different reinvestment rate assumptions.

To Better Understand the IRR of a Project, Ask Two Questions

To better understand the context of a stated IRR, **ask two questions**. First, ask, **"What is the assumed reinvestment rate?"** This question alone indicates whether the person presenting an investment idea is aware of or considered the reinvestment rate. Ideally, the person will respond, "we assumed that interim cash flows were reinvested at the cost of capital" or some other reasonable rate. Otherwise, the IRR may overstate the potential returns of the investment.

Second, ask, **"When do the interim cash flows occur in the life of the investment?"** With an improper reinvestment rate assumption, IRR's overstatement of potential returns will be larger when cash flows occur sooner rather than later. Why? Because the assumed reinvestment rate goes into effect sooner – it's applied early on generated cash flows – and the returns from this overstated IRR accumulate for more years. This is why the ideal project for applying IRR has one outgoing initial investment and one incoming cash flow at the end. In that case, IRR provides a perfect read on annualized returns.

Advantages and Disadvantages of Using IRR

What are key advantages and disadvantages from using IRR as an investment screen and capital budgeting criterion?

Advantages include:
- IRR uses cash flows.
- IRR accounts for the time value of money.
- IRR is intuitively easy to understand.

Disadvantages include:
- Real IRRs may not exist for "unconventional" and alternating positive and negative cash flows. In such cases, multiple IRRs are mathematically possible.
- IRR does not account for investment size. As a 'rate' of return, IRR is a relative measure; it does not speak to investment size or wealth creation. An IRR of 12% does not tell us if this applies to an

investment of $100 or $100 million. (This is why NPV and IRR are often applied in tandem.)

- Importantly, IRR can give unrealistic rates of return because of the reinvestment rate assumption; it assumes that all intermediate cash flows are reinvested at the IRR.

How and When Do NPV and IRR Complement and Conflict?

Answer:

NPV and IRR can provide conflicting guidance when comparing projects with different risk profiles and cash flow patterns. When this occurs, NPV offers the proper signal in all situations where maximizing value (wealth) is the goal. Regardless, both NPV and IRR provide insight when evaluating potential forestry investments.

Discussion and Example:

With potential investments, **IRR and NPV typically provide consistent guidance**, especially when evaluating individual projects with similar risk and timing of cash flows against a common discount rate. However, IRR can prove problematic in certain situations.

Consider two examples, one where NPV and IRR align, and another where we get inconsistent guidance. For the first, assume a forestry project with the following cash flows:

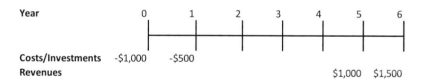

Using NPV, our decision to accept or reject the project depends on our discount rate. In the table below, we discount each cash flow to Year 0 using a range of rates. Then, we sum the discounted cash flows to estimate the NPV. We get positive NPVs for discount rates up to 10%. We estimate negative NPVs for discount rates or hurdle rates several basis points above this level.

Discount Rate	0	1	2	3	4	5	6	NPV
2%	-$1,000	-$490	$0	$0	$0	$906	$1,332	$747
4%	-$1,000	-$481	$0	$0	$0	$822	$1,185	$527
6%	-$1,000	-$472	$0	$0	$0	$747	$1,057	$333
8%	-$1,000	-$463	$0	$0	$0	$681	$945	$163
10%	-$1,000	-$455	$0	$0	$0	$621	$847	$13
12%	-$1,000	-$446	$0	$0	$0	$567	$760	-$119

Somewhere between 10% and 12% is the exact rate which delivers an NPV of zero. We find this rate is 10.2%; this is the IRR.

Per our investment criterion, NPV says to accept this project for discount rates of ~10% or less. Using IRR, we should accept this project if our discount rate is below 10.2%. In this case, both criteria provide consistent accept/reject signals.

At times, IRR and NPV give conflicting guidance. Consider a second example of two mutually exclusive projects with cash flows that differ in timing:

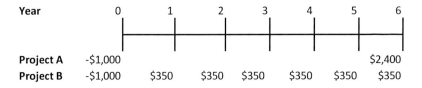

Year	0	1	2	3	4	5	6
Project A	-$1,000						$2,400
Project B	-$1,000	$350	$350	$350	$350	$350	$350

Both projects require $1,000 initial investments. Project A generates $2,400 in cash six years later. Project B generates $350 per year for six years, for a total cash inflow of $2,100. Project A generates more total cash, while Project B generates cash sooner.

In applying our investment criteria, we find IRRs of 15.7% for Project A and 26.4% for Project B. IRR indicates that Project B is preferable.

For a range of discount rates (table below), we find that the NPV for Project A exceeds Project B for low discount rates (at 3% in our example) and the NPV for Project B exceeds Project A for higher discount rates. When comparing the two, NPV prefers Project A for low hurdle rates and Project B for higher discount rates.

Discount Rate	NPV	
	Project A	Project B
3%	$ 1,010	$ 896
6%	$ 692	$ 721
9%	$ 431	$ 570
12%	$ 216	$ 439
15%	$ 38	$ 325
18%	$ (111)	$ 224
IRR	15.7%	26.4%

Higher rates severely "discount" the larger, delayed cash flow from Project A, while lower discount rates let the value of the Project A cash flow "stay ahead" of the Project B cash flows as they accumulate over time. This is the "time value of money" in action.

The key point is that **NPV uses the "actual" or "correct" cost of capital for the firm** (the chosen hurdle rate to discount cash flows). This rate is usually "risk-adjusted" to account for the relative riskiness of projects. IRR arbitrarily solves for the discount rate to make NPV equal to zero. In addition, NPV doesn't suffer from the IRR reinvestment rate issue detailed earlier. Finally, NPV lets us apply a range of discount rates to assess different levels of risk.

NPV or IRR?

NPV and IRR criteria use discounted cash flows to provide accept/reject signals for potential investments. In forestry, these criteria, at times, conflict when comparing projects with differences in timing, duration, and risk. These can, for example, include silvicultural treatments or harvest decisions. Generally, both NPV and IRR provide insight and should be estimated when evaluating potential forestry investments.

Which is better: NPV or IRR? In forest economics, NPV remains the preferred metric for investment analysis while IRR is recognized as the easier metric to understand and communicate. If the goal is to maximize wealth, NPV provides the superior signal when choosing between mutually exclusive investments. For a given investment size and pre-selected discount rate, NPV specifies which investment will generate greater wealth for the investor.

How and When Do We Use Bare Land Value (BLV)?

Answer:

Bare land value (BLV) allows us to compare forestry investments of different rotation lengths. BLV helps (1) identify the optimal rotation length; (2) order forest management activities; and (3) determine whether to invest in specific silvicultural activities.

Discussion and Example:

In 1849, Martin Faustmann read an article about forest valuation procedures and found it wanting. A German forester and appraiser, he developed and published an alternative technique for valuing bare forestland for tax purposes. Faustmann's approach uses prices, costs, and interest rates to determine the optimal economic forest rotation. Faustmann's formula – referred to as bare land value (BLV) or land expectation value (LEV) or soil expectation value (SEV) – remains the benchmark model for maximizing forest value through identifying the optimal timber rotation age.[3]

What makes BLV useful for evaluating forestry investments? While NPV and IRR work with single rotation investments, BLV is a special application of NPV that lets us compare forestry investments of different rotation lengths by assuming all costs and revenues are generated in perpetuity. BLV helps identify the forest rotation (age) that maximizes the value of the forest.

$$\text{BLV} = \frac{\text{Harvest Value at Rotation Age - Regen Costs} * (1 + \text{Rate})^{\text{Rotation Age}}}{(1 + \text{Rate})^{\text{Rotation Age}} - 1}$$

In the BLV formula above, "Harvest Value" refers to the volume harvested at final harvest multiplied by the appropriate stumpage values. "Regeneration Costs" refer to the investment made at the beginning of the rotation to get trees in the ground. "Rate" refers to the discount rate.

---

[3] In the 1990 S. J. Hall Lecture in Industrial Forestry at U.C. Berkeley, John Walker identified Faustmann's work as the "first known correct application of compound interest rates in discounted cash flow analyses." I am proud that a forester has such an important entrepreneurial place in the history of finance.

The BLV math includes two steps. First, it carries (compounds) each revenue and cost to the end of the rotation. Second, it applies a version of NPV to estimate value on a perpetual periodic basis.

BLV relies on key assumptions. First, **BLV assumes that costs and revenues for all future rotations remain identical.** This means known, constant prices and costs, and a constant discount rate. Second, **BLV assumes that the land will be reforested in perpetuity.** We don't include a land value in the BLV math; rather, BLV estimates the "bare land value" for us. Third, **BLV assumes that regeneration costs occur at the beginning of each rotation.**

Implications of BLV

In theory, **BLV represents the maximum you could pay to buy bare land at the beginning of a forest rotation** and earn the rate of return represented by the discount rate. When the estimated value for an alternative land use (such as development or row crops) exceeds the value for forestry as estimated by BLV, landowners have a financial justification and motivation to convert the land out of trees.

Faustmann, with BLV, captures the value of future forest rotations. Still, **the estimated BLV may not correspond to current market values for the land.** Investors may have alternative uses, in which case the forestry-centric BLV may not be competitive. Investors may also use different discount rates, which would produce different BLVs even with identical assumptions for costs and revenues.

In addition, different forest management strategies can result in different BLVs. The same forest can perform differently when managed by different owners.

Using BLV to Compare Forest Investment Strategies

BLV helps compare silvicultural strategies and forest investment options. If we rank alternate forest prescriptions using a single-rotation NPV, problems arise with different rotation lengths. Consider this case:

Forestry Investment	Duration (years)	NPV ($/acre)
Project A	20	$100
Project B	25	$90

Which forestry project would we choose? It's unclear. Since the projects have different durations, we need assumptions for reinvesting the income from the shorter investment (Project A) generated in year 20 to match the length of the longer 25-year investment (Project B). By matching time horizons, we can definitively compare the financial implications of the two projects.

A classic example has a forest owner in the U.S. South using BLV to compare a sawtimber management strategy to a pulpwood-focused strategy. The timelines below show these approaches:

Sawtimber Forest Management

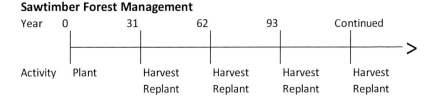

Pulpwood Forest Management

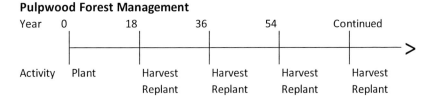

The sawtimber strategy – which might include intermediate cash flows from thinnings – grows trees with longer rotations into larger, more valuable logs used for lumber and plywood. The pulpwood strategy uses shorter rotations to grow large volumes of lower-valued trees for producing paper, energy, and engineered products.

BLV analysis using average timber prices and management costs could find the 31-year rotation sawtimber strategy generates $200 to $300 more in present value per acre to the landowner than a pulpwood strategy managed on 18-year rotations in local markets with healthy mills. In short, **BLV provides a way to compare the value creation of different strategies for the same tract of land within a given timber market.**

What Factors Affect Bare Land Values (BLV)?

BLV is the net present value of all revenues and costs associated with growing timber on a specific tract of land. BLV assumes this net value repeats as a perpetual series. Specific factors affect estimated bare land values, including:

- Site quality: foresters use the term "site" when speaking to the productive quality of land. Better quality sites have higher BLVs than poorer sites because they grow more timber volumes faster, which translate into higher expected cash flows from timber sales in the future.

- Costs: site preparation (site prep) and planting costs affect BLV because the first expense occurs immediately in year 0, and again at the start of each rotation. Annual costs such as property taxes and administration also affect BLV.

- Prices: projected timber yields and assumed timber prices determine the timber-related cash flows applied to the BLV math, so those prices matter.

- Silvicultural regime: the planned forest management strategy comprises a bundle of costs, forest growth expectations, and tree harvesting activities that determine the assumed wood flows and cash flows for this tract as managed by this owner.

- Discount rate: higher rates lower the present value of future expected cash flows, resulting in lower estimates of BLV, as well. Lower assumed discount rates do just the opposite.

What is the Relationship Between NPV and BLV?

The analysis below gives a sense for how NPV compares to BLV for a given forest. Data comes from a productive, intensively managed pine plantation in Georgia, which included chemical site preparation, herbaceous weed control, fertilization, and 500 trees planted per acre. The stand was thinned at age 12 and again at age 18. Based on a maximum BLV of $1,511 per acre, the optimal rotation was estimated at 28 years.

Year	Activity	NPV ($/acre)	% BLV
0	Plant		
28	Final harvest	$1,056	70%
56	Final harvest	$1,284	85%

The single-rotation NPV of $1,056 per acre for this stand captures 70% of the total BLV. Once we extend the analysis to include the second rotation, the NPV captures 85% of the estimated BLV.

In summary, **BLV provides the "theoretically" appropriate measure for valuing bare land managed exclusively for timber production.** BLV also provides the proper tool for comparing forest management strategies and for identifying the optimal forest rotation.

BLV is a guide. As a tool, **BLV supports financial decisions associated with forests.** It captures all opportunity costs associated with the land. Relative to NPV, it has advantages for estimating the impacts of alternate rotation lengths and forest management strategies. With BLV, we can maximize the value of a forest through identifying the rotation that achieves the highest value for different strategies.

Matching Financial Criteria to Forest Investment Questions

Choosing which financial criterion to apply for capital allocation decisions depends on the questions we're asking.

SUMMARY: Suggested Financial Criteria for Forest Investments

Question	Suggested Criteria to Prioritize
1. Accept/Reject: Does this project or forest investment satisfy our criteria?	• NPV and IRR • Note: BLV will provide a "signal" consistent with NPV and IRR
2. Rank/Prioritize: Of the qualifying projects or forest investments, which should we choose?	• NPV • BLV (and EAE)
3. Value/Valuation: What is this forest asset worth?	• NPV • BLV for the land; NPV for the timber
4. Optimize: How do we maximize the value of the timberland asset we own?	• BLV • NPV and IRR

Accept/Reject

When evaluating whether a specific investment satisfies basic discounted cash flow criteria, metrics such as NPV and IRR, as well as BLV, give consistent "accept/reject" signals. This is also true for marginal analysis questions related to, for example, incremental fertilizer treatments.

30

Observation: Applying NPV and IRR in tandem prudently deepens an analysis while improving the ability to communicate results to multiple audiences. Some folks want to see the dollars (NPV) while others prefer rates of return (IRR). Since the inputs needed to estimate both criteria overlap, the incremental work is negligible.

Rank/Prioritize

When ranking or prioritizing those forest investments which satisfy the basic criteria, NPV is recommended as it provides an "absolute" measure of wealth creation relative to a common discount rate. (In cases, BLV and Equal Annual Equivalent (EAE) also work well.) While IRR yields results consistent with NPV and BLV, it is not ideal as a standalone metric for ranking projects requiring significantly different initial investments because IRR provides a "relative" measure.

Observation: If choosing from financially acceptable, mutually exclusive investments, and capital is limited, apply NPV.

Value/Valuation

When valuing timberlands, appraisers rely heavily on sales comparisons or comparable sales (market "comps") and income approaches. The income approach requires estimates of future cash flows based on expected forest growth and stumpage prices, and the use of DCF models and analysis to estimate NPVs (and IRRs).

Observation: Valuing forest land often comprises the separate valuation of the forest and the land. BLV can support the estimation of land value for growing timber (though this estimate may deviate from local market values). In cases, timber valuation may not require DCF analysis; rather, estimating the liquidation value of harvesting all timber may be sufficient. For this, multiply product volumes by their current local timber market prices. (That's not a recommendation; it's just how it happens sometimes, especially for smaller tracts.)

Optimize

To estimate the optimal rotation or forest management strategy, prioritize the use of bare land value (BLV). EAE is also applicable. NPV and IRR also work well for a range of screening and ranking forest investment projects.

Observation: At times, the optimal rotation age differs when estimated with NPV versus BLV. Why? The optimal rotation is longer with NPV because subsequent stands, and the future regeneration costs, are not considered. BLV assumes an infinite series of rotations, resulting in a shorter optimal rotation age than NPV alone. Since BLV includes all future cash flows, it's the most comprehensive and complete criterion for optimizing the rotation age.

In practice, applying and accepting BLV requires nuance. If BLV and your analysis determine that the optimal forest rotation is 26 years, you will find that the BLV and NPV are 'flat' in the years before and after year 26. While the forest might be considered financially mature at age 26, from an investment standpoint, it won't differ much if the trees are harvested at age 24 or 28. The prevailing market conditions and timber prices, and your budget situation, will provide better signals and motivators about whether to harvest "now" versus waiting for the theoretical optimal age in a spreadsheet.

Examples and Cases Using NPV, IRR, and BLV

We learn by doing. **This section includes brief examples and cases for practicing the application of NPV, IRR, and BLV**. Often, we have different ways to analyze an investment. Here, we emphasize a simple, systematic approach to strengthen skills and minimize errors.

First, **specify the question** ("what is the question?"). Value-added analysis or research starts by clarifying a question to answer and the audience we're preparing this for. Our analysis helps the person making a decision, and if they don't agree on the question or understand the analysis, we've done nothing useful.

Second, **apply the appropriate formula** to answer the question. Deciding which financial criterion to use depends on the question asked. When evaluating whether a specific investment satisfies basic DCF criteria, certain questions may favor one metric over another.

Third, **check the results**. What do they mean? Do the numbers make sense? Through checking results consistently over time, we develop a sense for ranges and logic, which improves our general fluency and intuition in forestry and finance.

Example: Present Value of a Forest Thinning

You expect to generate $850 per acre from thinning your forest in 15 years. What is the Present Value of this revenue assuming a 7% discount rate?

First, confirm the question. In this example, we anticipate $850 in cash revenue per acre from thinning our forest 15 years in the future. The question is, "what is the value today (present value) of the $850 earned in 15 years assuming a discount rate (opportunity cost) of 7%?"

Second, choose and apply the appropriate formula. The question asks about present value, which is the discounted value to today of cash received in the future:

$$
\begin{aligned}
\textit{Present Value} \quad &= \textit{Future Value}/(1 + \textit{rate})^n \\
&= \$850/(1 + .07)^{15} \\
&= \$850/(1.07)^{15} \\
&= \$308.08
\end{aligned}
$$

Finally, we review the results and confirm we understand what they mean. Based on the math, the answer to our question is, "the value today of $850 received 15 years in the future discounted at 7% is $308."

To build intuition, we take another moment to appreciate (or feel dismayed by) the impact of discounting. Picture the $850 earned in 15 years shrinking 7% each and every year.

Since 7% of $850 is $59.50, that means the value fell to $790.50 in the first year of discounting, from year 15 to year 14.

In the next year, from year 14 to 13, the $790.50 decreased another 7%, or $55.34, to $735.17.

And so on.

In this case, there is no "net" present value or internal rate of return (IRR) to estimate because there was no initial investment. IRR is the average rate of appreciation on the initial dollars invested over the project life that makes the NPV equal to zero. A project with no initial investment will have an infinite IRR, which means nothing. The question here simply asks what money received in the future would be worth in today's dollars.

Example: Financial Analysis of a Fertilizer Treatment

Your consulting forester recommends a mid-rotation fertilizer treatment for your 14-year-old, recently thinned loblolly pine plantation. The treatment would cost $80 per acre. Should you consider this investment?

This common forest management situation has a couple of parts. To start, we specify the question. In this case, we can choose one of two approaches.

The first is, "*what is the expected rate of return from investing in the fertilizer treatment?*" This requires information of expected forest growth and timber prices by product, in addition to an assumed discount rate and time horizon. It requires the expected cash flows (from the consulting forester or forest model) to analyze rates of return.

The second type of question focuses on a break-even analysis, and asks, "*what would be the minimum required cash flow from this investment to satisfy our opportunity costs?*" This approach simply needs the analyst to choose a discount rate and confirm the time horizon. It provides context for the investment opportunity.

In this case, let's draft the question for the break-even analysis to capture key assumptions related to discount rates and time horizons:

Assuming a 6% discount rate and a final harvest in ten years at age 24, how much incremental revenue per acre makes this investment a break-even proposition?

The question speaks to return on investment. Will it generate enough return on the $80 per acre over the next ten years to cover our 6% opportunity cost? To answer, we apply the future value formula to see how much revenue we'd need to generate from the $80 investment to make this worthwhile.

$$
\begin{aligned}
\textit{Future Value} \quad &= \textit{Present Value} * (1 + rate)^n \\
&= \$80 * (1 + .06)^{10} \\
&= \$80 * (1.06)^{10} \\
&= \$143.27
\end{aligned}
$$

This means the fertilizer treatment needs to generate $143 per acre of incremental revenue ten years from now (or sooner) to justify the $80 investment. In other words, generating $143 in 10 years means we would earn 6% per year on the $80 invested today.

The $143 incremental cash per acre ten years from now becomes our floor. This **break-even test is a form of sensitivity analysis** that can be used later to determine how much forest growth or timber prices can vary from our assumptions while still allowing the fertilizer treatment to pay for itself.

When communicating results, I find break-even analysis often helps investors, executives, Boards of Directors, and others better think through questions and concerns related to downside risk.

Now, let's evaluate the expected financial performance of the fertilizer investment. First, confirm the question:

What are the expected NPV and IRR of the fertilizer treatment, assuming a 6% discount rate and a ten-year investment period?

To answer, we apply formulas for net present value (NPV) and internal rate of return (IRR). We also need an estimate of the future expected cash flow, which requires information on incremental forest growth from fertilizing, and assumptions related to timber prices.

Our consulting forester expects the treatment to grow an incremental 40 or more tons per acre over the ten years, and he expects at least half of that volume to be higher-valued grade logs and the balance to be lower-valued pulpwood. He provides a range of potential outcomes for our analysis.

In a spreadsheet, we organize the inputs – the fertilizer cost, discount rate, time horizon, and assumed log prices ($20/ton for grade and $10/ton for pulpwood) – and use them with the NPV and IRR formulas to estimate a set of results.

Fertilizer cost, $/acre	$80
Discount rate, %	6%
Time to harvest, years	10
Grade logs, $/ton	$20
Pulpwood, $/ton	$10

Tons/acre	% Grade	Revenue/acre	NPV	IRR
30	50%	$450	$171.28	18.9%
40	40%	$560	$232.70	21.5%
40	50%	$600	$255.04	22.3%
40	60%	$640	$277.37	23.1%
50	50%	$750	$338.80	25.1%

Now, let's check the numbers to confirm our understanding. For example, look at the middle, outlined set of results: 40 tons/acre with 50% grade generates $600 per acre (20 tons of $20/ton grade logs + 20 tons of $10/ton pulpwood logs). That $600 discounted 10 years at 6% gives an NPV of $255, which represents a 22.3% IRR on the $80 fertilizer investment. Pretty good!

Does this use of cash satisfy our financial opportunity costs? The positive NPV means we earned an additional $255 per acre of present value above that required to break even on our $80 investment. The 22.3% IRR far exceeds the discount rate. The analysis indicates that, yes, we should consider this investment.

In addition, compare the range of incremental revenues/acre to our previous break-even analysis. The future cash flows from fertilizing exceed by hundreds of dollars the $143 break-even floor. Both parts of our analysis tell a consistent story.

Case: Ten-Year Timberland Investment

A forest manager pools funds from four individuals for a 1,000-acre, ten-year timberland investment. Given the proposed management plan below, what are the expected NPV and IRR using a 7% discount rate?

Quartet Investments plans to acquire a 1,000-acre timberland property on behalf of four individual investors to execute a strategy of (1) generating periodic cash flows while (2) growing quality, mature sawtimber. The plan expects to generate most of its returns through offering to the market in ten years a property with over 50% of the acres ready or nearly ready to harvest and generate cash.

The Quarter Investments management plan for the forest includes the following elements and assumptions:

- Acquire the property for a maximum of $2,500 per acre.
- In years 2 and 6, harvest 200 acres of mature timber, generating $400,000 of net revenue each time.
- In years 3 and 7, site prep and replant the 200 harvested acres at a cost of $250 per acre.
- At the end of each year, pay $6 per acre in property management fees and $8 per acre for property taxes.
- Sell the land and timber after 10 years for at least $3,800 per acre.

The expectation with the management plan is that, at the time of sale, 60% of the property will have mature or nearly mature timber, while the balance of the acres will have been reforested.

Quartet Investments Ten-Year Timberland Fund

Assumptions		
Acres	1,000	
Purchase price	$ 2,400	per acre
Hunting leases	10	per acre per year
Property taxes	8	per acre per year
Property management	6	per acre per year
Selling price	$ 3,800	per acre
Discount rate	7.0%	

Financial Analysis		
Total NPV	$ 47,593	
NPV	$ 48	per acre
IRR	7.2%	

Annual Cash Flows

Year	0	1	2	3	4	5	6	7	8	9	10
Revenue											
Timber Sales			$ 400,000				$ 400,000				
Hunting leases		$ 10,000	$ 10,000	$ 10,000	$ 10,000	$ 10,000	$ 10,000	$ 10,000	$ 10,000	$ 10,000	$ 10,000
Total Revenue		$ 10,000	$ 410,000	$ 10,000	$ 10,000	$ 10,000	$ 410,000	$ 10,000	$ 10,000	$ 10,000	$ 10,000
Expenses											
Management Fees		$ 6,000	$ 6,000	$ 6,000	$ 6,000	$ 6,000	$ 6,000	$ 6,000	$ 6,000	$ 6,000	$ 6,000
Taxes		$ 8,000	$ 8,000	$ 8,000	$ 8,000	$ 8,000	$ 8,000	$ 8,000	$ 8,000	$ 8,000	$ 8,000
Total Expenses		$ 14,000	$ 14,000	$ 14,000	$ 14,000	$ 14,000	$ 14,000	$ 14,000	$ 14,000	$ 14,000	$ 14,000
Cash Flow											
Operating Income	$ -	$ (4,000)	$ 396,000	$ (4,000)	$ (4,000)	$ (4,000)	$ 396,000	$ (4,000)	$ (4,000)	$ (4,000)	$ (4,000)
Reforestation Expense				$ 50,000				$ 50,000			
Cap Ex: Acquisitions	$ 2,400,000										
Cap Ex: Divestitures											$ 3,800,000
Total Cash Flow	$ (2,400,000)	$ (4,000)	$ 396,000	$ (54,000)	$ (4,000)	$ (4,000)	$ 396,000	$ (54,000)	$ (4,000)	$ (4,000)	$ 3,796,000
Present Value Analysis											
PV of Cash Flows	$ (2,400,000)	$ (3,738)	$ 345,882	$ (44,080)	$ (3,052)	$ (2,852)	$ 263,872	$ (33,628)	$ (2,328)	$ (2,176)	$ 1,929,694

The financial analysis in the plan estimates the NPV with a 7% discount rate and calculates the IRR given the assumed cash flows. We review the numbers to confirm that the assumptions and timing of the cash flows match the plan.

Then we spend a few minutes checking the math. The outgoing cash flows total $2.64 million, which include $2.4 million to acquire the property, $100,000 in reforestation expenses, and $14,000 per year for ten years in annual expenses. The incoming cash flows total $4.7 million, which include $3.8 million for the sale, $800,000 in net harvest revenues, and $10,000 per year in annual hunting lease income.

What do the financial results tell us? Do they make sense given those cash flows? The 7.2% IRR, the discount rate that makes the NPV equal zero, just exceeds our discount rate of 7%, which means the modest NPV of $48 per acre is logical.

Example: Your Neighbor Sells Some Forestland

A neighbor offers to sell you 40 acres of adjoining forestland that will be ready to harvest in about eight years. Your forester thinks the timber and land will be worth about $2,700 per acre at that time. If your discount rate (opportunity cost) is 5%, what would you be willing to pay for this land per acre today?

First, confirm the question:

What is the present value today of $2,700 assuming a 5% discount rate and an eight-year investment period?

Second, we apply the present value formula:

Present Value = *Future Value/(1 + rate)^n*
$$= \$2,700/(1 + .05)^8$$
$$= \$1,827.47$$

Third, you check the results. Discounting $2,700 at 5% for 8 years is the mirror of taking $1,827 and investing at 5% for 8 years. You decide to take a closer look at the property and see if the neighbor will accept $1,750 per acre while discussing the matter over a cold beer.

SIDEBAR: How Do I Value a Forest?

The basic process for valuing timberlands requires collecting forest and market data, modeling forest growth and yields, and conducting a DCF analysis of estimated cash flows. The steps include:

1. Characterize the current forest. Quantify (cruise) the current volume and inventory by product and specie, and capture other information required to generate a growth and yield model (e.g., site index, acres). Then, collect data on markets, hauling distances, and logging costs that further clarify the realizable market value and operating costs.

2. Generate a growth and yield model of the forest. Also called a "forest estate model", this projects the harvest volumes (yields) by product and year over the investment period.

3. Build a DCF model to project cash flows. This nets future revenues against costs to initiate the valuation process. Harvest revenues will include assumptions related to timber prices and alternate income sources such as hunting leases. Costs will include silvicultural expenses, management fees, property taxes, etc. Finally, the DCF model requires a discount rate, which may correspond to a client's hurdle rate or cost of capital.

4. Identify the optimum economic rotation for the forest. Using the DCF model, we can identify the rotation age that maximizes BLV. This also helps determine the optimal forest management strategy for the forest as we can compare different approaches.

5. Estimate the NPV based on the investment horizon. This will require a terminal value for exiting the investment that would be based on the expected forest inventory at the end of the investment period, in addition to an assumed value for the land.

6. Conduct a sensitivity analysis. Test key assumptions related to the discount rate, harvest yields, stumpage forecasts, and costs.

How Can We Value an Uneven-Aged Forest?

Answer:
Valuing an uneven-aged forest managed in perpetuity is simply another application of BLV. For investments of finite duration, we can use NPV.

Discussion and Example:

Forest stands with uneven-aged timber comprise diverse age classes that distinguish themselves from plantations with stands of even aged trees. Uneven-aged forests are often managed on cycles of periodic partial harvests that remove select, mature trees. Since the stand is "never" clear cut, the stand is never replanted in the sense we're used to for estimating BLVs.

Consider an uneven-aged forest managed on five or ten-year cutting cycles. Under this strategy, we harvest selected, financially mature trees every five or ten years. The steps required to value this stand include:

1. Estimating the volume and product mix harvested each cycle.
   a. It is common to apply average per-acre growth rates by product. Since the uneven-aged management strategy prioritizes financially mature timber, the harvest mix would be primarily sawtimber with a small portion allocated to culled trees removed opportunistically.
2. Applying per unit prices to these products.
   a. This may use a stand or market-specific forecast, or long-term averages by product and specie.
3. Calculating NPV (for fixed duration investments) or BLV for the value of perpetual, periodic costs, and revenues.

Secondary Financial Criteria: EAE, Cash-on-Cash, Payback, and More

At times, investors and analysts employ other financial criteria, some of which are commonly used in manufacturing or other sectors with shorter investment periods. **This chapter covers several of these criteria and discusses the pros and cons for applying them to forest investments,** in addition to answering topical questions such as:

- How and when do we use equal annual equivalent (EAE)?
- When do I use cash-on-cash (COC) returns in forestry?
- What are payback period and discounted payback period?
- When is the "current stand" approach useful to value forestland?
- When is the "current rotation" approach useful?

How and When Do We Use Equal Annual Equivalent (EAE)?

Answer:

Equal annual equivalent (EAE) provides a measure of annual profitability that can compare investments of different duration, such as multi-year timber investments and annual agriculture crops. EAE turns NPV into a series of equal annual cash flows; it is the project's NPV stated as an annual payment.

Discussion and Examples:

Having a measure of annual profitability can be useful. Equal annual equivalent (EAE) – also called equivalent annual cash (EAC) flows or equivalent annual annuity (EAA) or equal annual income – provides a measure for comparing projects of different duration or "economic lives." EAE can help compare multi-year timber investments with other potential investments that generate annual cash flows such as bonds or agricultural crops. The approach, like BLV, assumes that the projects continue forever (live in perpetuity).

Calculating EAE has three steps:

1. Estimate the NPV of each investment for one period (such as one forest rotation).
2. Calculate the EAE of each project (using the formula below), which provides the annual payment that equals the estimated NPV with the assumed discount rate.

3. Compare and choose the project with the highest EAE.

$$EAE = \frac{Rate * NPV}{1 - (1 + Rate)^{-Years}}$$

For example, assume a firm is comparing two projects. Project A has an NPV of $100 and a life of 10 years, while Project B has an NPV of $50 and a life of 5 years. Our firm has an 8% cost of capital.

Project A EAE $= (0.08 * \$100)/[1 - (1.08)^{-10}]$
$= \$14.90$

Project B EAE $= (0.08 * \$50)/[1 - (1.08)^{-5}]$
$= \$12.52$

The math of EAE indicates that Project A "earns" $14.90 per year or present value above the 8% discount rate while Project B generates $12.52 on an annual basis. Per the decision rule, the firm should choose Project A.

In sum, EAE spreads equally the benefits of each investment over the investments' life spans. It compares potential investments and shows their NPVs as series of equal annual cash flows, given a cost of capital. Like NPV, the EAE decision rule for independent projects says accept those with positive EAEs and reject those that are negative. Like BLV, EAE helps compare investment alternatives that have unequal timelines.

When is EAE Helpful for Evaluating Forestry Investments?

EAE helps compare investments that generate periodic returns (e.g. forestry) with those that produce annual returns (e.g. agriculture or other real estate).

Consider the case of helping a landowner choose the most productive use of her 100-acre pasture. The land has been in her family for years and she plans to keep it managed as a working forest or farm, depending on the results of the analysis.

You call an agriculture extension specialist for the income per acre per year available to landowners from growing soybeans in this county. He estimates – based on regional farm budgets and long-term averages for soybean prices and yields – an annual per acre net income from growing soybeans of $60 per acre.

Then you analyze the EAE of planting the 100-acre pasture in pine trees managed on a 24-year rotation. The landowner's discount rate is 6%. Following the three steps, you find:
1. NPV of one pine sawtimber rotation = $900.
2. EAE of one pine sawtimber rotation =
   a. $(0.06 * \$900)/[1 – (1.06)^{-24}] = \$71.71$
3. $71.71 EAE of pine sawtimber exceeds the $60 annual net income of soybeans for this land in this area.

Based on this analysis, the landowner chooses to plant the pasture in trees and grow sawtimber.[4]

When Do I Use Cash-on-Cash Returns to Value Timberlands?

Answer:

The use of **cash-on-cash returns** as a performance metric for timberland investments has narrow applications.

Discussion and Example:

Most reported returns from timberland investments reflect unrealized "paper" gains. Timberland indices and appraisals have limitations, complicating efforts to check the status of active timber investments. This spotlights hard measures – like cash – to assess performance. **Investors new to timberland assets often ask about cash-on-cash returns as a point of comparison**. However, a meaningful timber analysis benchmarks cash flows relative to future expectations, not just the current year.

Cash-on-cash return (COCR) is a measure – a percentage – often used by investors for income-producing real estate. It is calculated by dividing before-tax cash flow by the amount of cash invested (down payment amount). If before-tax cash flow for an investment property is $15,000 and our invested cash is $100,000, then cash-on-cash return is 15% ($15K/$100K).

---

[4] You can convert a bare land value (BLV) to an EAE by multiplying the BLV by the discount rate. For example, if the BLV of a pine plantation is $1,200 per acre assuming a 6% discount rate, then the per acre EAE would be $1,200 * .06 = $72. [Note: the BLV for an NPV of $900 from our example is $1,195.17, which is the EAE of $71.71.]

$$\text{Cash-on-Cash Return} = \frac{\text{Annual Dollar Income}}{\text{Total Dollar Investment}}$$

The "annual dollar income" is the cash flow the property is expected to generate during the first year of operation. The "total dollar investment" is the total cash invested to acquire the property including down payment, loan points, title fees, appraisals, and inspection costs. It can also be shown as:

$$\text{Cash-on-Cash Return} = \frac{\text{Net Cash Flow}}{\text{Invested Equity}}$$

Timberland investors naturally care about the cash flows and distributions from their investments. These cash flows vary with the products grown, markets served, and age distribution of the forest owned. Also, timberland portfolios can be constructed to meet a range of cash flow objectives. That said, the use of COCR as a performance metric for timberland investments has narrow applications, if any.

While COCR provides one way for real estate investors to quickly compare the profitability of income-producing properties, it has limits. **COCR does not account for the time value of money**. Cash-on-cash return functions well for measuring a property's first year cash flow but not its future year's cash flows, where each successive year becomes increasingly speculative.

Also, **COCR does not account for appreciation**. Lower COCR today may offer a greater opportunity for appreciation than acquiring a property with steady COCR and little or no appreciation. For timber, a thorough analysis accounts for how growth rates differ by age; the pace of appreciation varies as forests grow and move through higher product classes in changing markets over time.

To better understand the limitations of COCR for timberland investments, assume we manage a forest on a 28-year rotation with a thinning at age 18 and final harvest at age 28. Any given ten-year ownership of this property produces many alternate return and cash flow scenarios.

Year	Cash Flows	Type	Returns
0-1	Site preparation	Cost	
	Seedlings	Cost	Negative cash flows
	Planting	Cost	
18	Pulpwood, Chip-n-saw	Revenue	Appreciation
	Biomass	Revenue	Moderate cash flows
	Hunting leases	Revenue	
28	Pulpwood, Chip-n-saw, Sawlogs	Revenue	Appreciation
	Biomass	Revenue	Strong cash flows
	Hunting leases	Revenue	

Owning a young forest may require investment and relies on expected appreciation and future cash flows. Owning a mid-term forest generates modest cash flows from early harvesting and thinning. A mature, well-stocked stand generates immediate, robust cash flows that reflect 28 years of growth and productivity. **While an investor can expect positive returns regardless the age, the source of those returns, and the nature of the cash flows, change over time.**

NOTE: What is the Difference Between ROI and COCR?

How does return on investment (ROI) differ from COCR? Assume you acquire a timberland tract for $500,000 and sell it later for $550,000:

Your return on investment (ROI) is 10%. The 10% return ($50,000 increase on $500,000 invested) reflects the increase in your "total investment (Loan + Cash Down Payment)."

If you put down 50% ($250,000), not accounting for closing costs and commissions, your cash-on-cash return (COCR) is 20%. The return you made on invested cash is 20% ($50,000 increase on $250,000 cash invested).

If you paid all cash for the tract, then COCR and ROI are equal.

What are "Payback Period" and "Discounted Payback Period"?

Payback period is the time, usually stated in years, required to recover the initial investment in a project. To calculate, sum incoming cash flows over time until recouping the investment. If we invest $100 today into a project that generates $25 per year, our payback period would be 4 years (25+25+25+25=100).

Alternately, discounted payback period discounts future cash flows which reduces their present value. In this way, discounted payback period estimates the number of years needed to "break even" on a capital investment. It differs from "normal" payback period, which disregards the time value of money to estimate the years required to cover initial investments.

To estimate the discounted payback period:
1. Select a discount rate.
2. Estimate the present value of each cash inflow from the project using this discount rate.
3. Sum the discounted cash flows over time until we recoup our investment.

The table shows how the payback period of 4 years from our example translates into a discounted payback period of 6 years assuming a 10% discount rate. By considering the time value of money, we extend the payback period.

Initial Investment	$100
Discount Rate	10%
Annual Cash Flow	$25

Year	Cash Flow	Discounted	Cumulative CF	Cumulative Discounted CF
1	$25	$23	$25	$23
2	$25	$21	$50	$43
3	$25	$19	$75	$62
4	$25	$17	$100	$79
5	$25	$16		$95
6	$25	$14		$109

Can a project with a negative NPV have a discounted payback period? No. In such cases, the cash inflows never "catch up" to repay the initial investment. Also, discounted payback period may reject positive NPV projects, as the metric is somewhat arbitrary and biased against longer-term projects.

Investors sometimes defend payback period as helpful for measuring risk because projected cash flows beyond three or four years are speculative. Also, corporate analysts defend payback period as useful for comparing projects, especially at manufacturing facilities, when capital is scarce.

When is the "Current Stand" Approach Useful to Value Forests?

Answer:
When talking about timberland investing while having a beer or standing over the hood of a truck, not when signing checks or allocating capital for long-term investing. The **"current stand approach" serves short-term investors looking to liquidate the asset upon purchase**, not as a comprehensive method for valuing timberland.

Discussion:
A reasonable estimate of a forest's current economic value equals the **standing merchantable volume multiplied by the current stumpage prices** in the local market. This "back-of-the-envelope" technique helps estimate the liquidation value of a timberland investment. However, this approach suffers from observable, value-destroying limitations. It **ignores the potential for generating greater wealth** by holding the forest to economic maturity, investing in forest management, identifying other income streams, or accounting for taxes or opportunity costs associated with the land and capital.

This snapshot value faces other weaknesses. First, current realizable values for the standing timber will be low at any given point in time. Also, for large timberland ownerships, the local market can rarely absorb a total liquidation (clear cut) of inventory without depressing local prices. Generally, appraisers valuing forests avoid current stand valuations (in writing).

The "current stand approach" serves short-term investors looking to liquidate the asset upon purchase. If you've heard someone say, "the forest paid for the land," it's likely they bought a forested property, harvested the trees, and covered their entire acquisition price with revenues generated from selling those trees.

What is the "Current Rotation" Approach to Valuing Forests?

The "current rotation" approach values a timberland property as equal to the net present value (NPV) of the first or current rotation. In cases where estimated values for future rotations beyond the current stand prove highly uncertain or irregular, this approach might be useful or interesting. Valuation models sometimes include future rotations that generate mind-numbing returns or cringe-worthy losses (and the "red flag" goes up so fast you hope it doesn't poke you in the eye).

Mathematically, the current rotation approach often aligns with decision criteria and guidance provided by multi-rotational or bare land value (BLV) analyses. For example, the NPV of a 25-year rotation forest will comprise approximately 70% of the estimated BLV. Therefore, if you live by the "80/20 rule" – the Pareto Principle which states that approximately 80% of the effects for a given event come from 20% of the causes – then a current rotation assessment may provide sufficient guidance for deciding on certain investments.

Finally, when applying the current rotation approach, we need to specify a terminal value. In practice, we can use the BLV as the estimate of selling the bare timberland at the end of the current rotation after the final harvest.

Marginal Analysis and Intermediate Harvest Decisions

We use marginal analysis to assess forest management and intermediate harvest decisions for existing stands. It answers questions of "when to harvest?" and "when does forest management pay?"

A timberland investor once told me, "You only get to cut a tree once." He made the point that, "our trees are in the ground already. So, how do we maximize the value of the forests we have?"

With marginal analysis, we compare the incremental costs and revenues of potential projects, investments, or one-off decisions. "Incremental" refers to the extra costs and revenues associated with the opportunity. To evaluate potential forest investments or harvest decisions, marginal analysis employs the full set of financial tools, including NPV, IRR, and BLV.

This section introduces key concepts, with examples, related to marginal analysis in forestry.

What are the Basic Steps for Marginal Analysis?

Answer:

Key steps include capturing the direct costs and benefits in a discounted cash flow metric such as NPV, IRR, or BLV. Direct costs include the capital (or cash) and opportunity costs, as reflected in the discount rate. The benefits can include, for example, increased value or revenues from growing more, higher quality timber during the investment life.

Discussion and Example:

In forest management and timberland investing, we evaluate potential activities based on the question, "how will this affect the value and returns of our timberland?" The analysis "on the margin" to answer this question includes:

1. Establish the baseline for the current forest. This has two parts.
   a. Cruise the current stand to estimate its volume and value.
   b. Produce a growth and yield projection of the current forest to estimate future harvest volumes.
2. Estimate a second growth and yield model that assumes the silviculture activity under consideration has been completed.

a. We would expect this second projection to generate more volume, or higher valued volume, than the baseline (if not, we're wasting time).
3. Net the volumes from the baseline projection against the second growth and yield model to quantify the benefit from the silviculture activity.
4. Quantify the value gain and returns associated with this additional volume using NPV, IRR, and/or BLV.
    a. This accounts for the costs, revenues, and opportunity costs of the silviculture treatment.

Marginal analysis costs are straightforward. They include the cash costs (expenses) of the activity, fees associated with obtaining cruises or other services, and carrying (capitalizing) the initial investments over time (opportunity cost).

Estimating the benefits (revenues) can prove challenging, as we work to specify the gains directly attributable to the new silviculture activity. The estimated benefit reflects the change in value between the treated and untreated forest.

Evaluating marginal or additional investments is common practice for capital budgeting for real assets, where these projects lead to increased productivity or profitability. With forests, the marginal investment usually relates to additional silviculture treatments that support increased growth rates and additional timber revenues and value.

EXAMPLE: Marginal Analysis of Mid-Rotation Fertilization

Let's apply the basic steps to the question of whether to fertilize a forest. Using data from a large mid-rotation study at North Carolina State University (NCSU) on loblolly pines, we can estimate the financial performance of fertilizer treatments.

NCSU researchers installed a series of forest plots. Some were fertilized; some were not. After eight years, NCSU measured the fertilized and unfertilized stands, providing a baseline and a range of net gains specific to mid-rotation fertilizer treatments.

The table below summarizes, in tons per acre, the marginal gain – the response specific to the fertilizer treatments – every two years following the fertilizer application. Looking at the "mean" responses, we see that growth slows after year six, gaining less than one ton (from 12 to 12.8 tons) over the final two years. Note: these studies by NCSU are a key reason why foresters in the U.S. South talk about how optimizing fertilizer treatments requires, plus or minus, six years.

| | Growth Response (tons/acre) | | | |
| | Age since fertilization (years) | | | |
Response	2	4	6	8
min	1.8	3.5	7.1	7.5
mean	2.2	4.9	12	12.8
max	3	7.2	15.1	16.2

To quantify the value gain and financial returns of these results, we apply costs, prices, and opportunity costs. Assume a discount rate of 7%, a stumpage price of $25 per ton, and fertilizer costs of $80 per acre.

First, we estimate the NPV gain per acre specific to the mid-rotation fertilizer treatments. For example, estimating the NPV of the mean response six years after the fertilizer treatment includes the following math:

$$NPV = -\$80 + [(12 \ tons * \$25)/[(1.07)^6]$$
$$= -\$80 + [(\$300)/[(1.07)^6]$$
$$= \$119.90 \ per \ acre$$

| | Net Present Value ($/acre) | | | |
| | Age since fertilization (years) | | | |
Response	2	4	6	8
min	$ (40.70)	$ (13.25)	$ 38.28	$ 29.13
mean	$ (31.31)	$ 13.45	$ 119.90	$ 106.24
max	$ (15.37)	$ 57.32	$ 171.54	$ 155.71

Based on the NPV analysis, assuming we achieve an average (mean) or better growth response, the mid-rotation fertilizer treatments generate positive value for anything at four years or beyond. NPV starts declining beyond year six, indicating the marginal benefit of the treatment slows to a rate below the discount rate.

Next, we estimate IRRs to complement the NPV analysis.

	Internal Rate of Return (%)			
	Age since fertilization (years)			
Response	2	4	6	8
min	-25.0%	2.3%	14.2%	11.2%
mean	-17.1%	11.2%	24.6%	18.9%
max	-3.2%	22.5%	29.5%	22.5%

IRR estimates affirm the NPV analysis, with strong, positive IRRs for anything at four years or beyond. The IRR also starts to decline beyond year six, indicating the marginal benefit of the treatment has slowed.

When Do We Harvest Timber to Maximize Financial Returns?

Answer:
We harvest timber when we maximize the present value of the current forest stand in combination with the future (subsequent) stands as reflected in the BLV.

Discussion:
"Should I harvest now, or wait for markets to improve?" This is a common question from forest owners. While many factors affect this, including forest health, our focus here is financial.

As a forest grows, it increases in value from (1) volume growth and (2) product advancement. Overall, we want to harvest at times that maximize the financial returns to the owner, even if that requires delaying a scheduled timber harvest.

Forest owners and managers face a range of intermediate harvest decisions that deviate from their original plans. Questions with financial implications may include:

- How do we analyze financial returns as timber markets change?
- How do we decide whether to clear cut for pulpwood or manage for sawtimber?
- How do we decide whether to harvest sawtimber now or wait for stronger markets?

The use of BLV helps us evaluate marginal harvest decisions. BLV captures the value of managing the forest under a specific strategy in perpetuity. It provides a baseline value that reflects all subsequent rotations. If we harvest today, the BLV captures our future forest. If we wait and harvest the current stand in two years, the BLV, discounted back two years, once again represents the value of putting the forest back to work under our forest management strategy.

The decision rule we can use to evaluate intermediate harvest decisions includes two components and one assessment.

- First, we need the NPV of harvesting the existing stand.
- Second, we need the BLV, which represents all future forests, discounted back from the year we harvest the intermediate stand.
- Then we add these two together.

We do this math and assess the change in value year-by-year. Once the growth in total value peaks, we harvest. When this total value begins to decline, it indicates that total forest value is growing at a rate below our discount rate.

Ideally, we want to avoid speculative handwringing over decisions on the margin (or any decision). BLV, like any metric, provides a tool to organize our thinking with the information we have at the time. If the math beats what you "should" get, don't worry about what you "could" get; go ahead and move forward. The decision makes you money relative to expectation (as measured by BLV).

EXAMPLE: Assessing the Value of a Post-Thin Cruise

Each decision to buy or sell an asset or service is, in some way, a marginal investment. This includes activities that assess the quality and performance of forest management. Management forester Jamie McKinnon and I reviewed the value of post-thin cruises. Forest thinnings increase forest productivity and value by removing weaker trees to concentrate resources on the highest potential, healthiest trees.

A post-thin cruise helps address two questions. One, was the thinning performed to specification? Two, if the thinning was conducted poorly, or if the stand is of low quality, should we let the forest grow to term or do we clear cut and replant to start over?

How can we test the value of an intensive post-thin cruise? Consider a case with two scenarios. We thin a forest at age 18 and plan a final harvest for age 25. The management plan indicates that we will also grow all subsequent forests on 25-year rotations.

In Scenario One, we grow the forest to age 25, but find that the stand was of poor quality, responded poorly to the thinning, and generated below average volumes and revenues at final harvest.

In Scenario Two, we conduct an intensive post-thin cruise and identify the forest quality issue. We clear cut the 18-year-old stand and replant to manage a new stand on 25-year sawtimber rotations.

The timelines below depict these two scenarios:

Scenario One: Thin and Harvest "On Schedule"

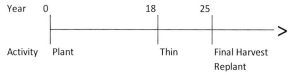

Scenario Two: Conduct Post-Thin Cruise and Start Over

How do we compare these scenarios to test the value gained or lost from the post-thin cruise? We first gather inputs for the analysis:

- BLV of our normal 25-year rotation sawtimber strategy.
    - We would have this from determining the optimal 25-year rotation in the first place. For this example, assume a bare land value (BLV) of $1,000 per acre.
- NPV of harvesting the poor-quality stand at age 25.
    - Discount an estimate of the final harvest revenue seven years from 25 to age 18, when we conducted the thin. For this example, assume we expect to generate $1,200 of revenue at final harvest. Discounting this at 6% for 7 years would be: $1,200/(1.06)^7 = $798 per acre.
- Cash flow of harvesting the poor stand at age 18 after the cruise.
    - Since we are at year 18, no discounting is required. Assume a clear-cut revenue of $500 per acre at age 18.
- Cost of the post-thin cruise.

- o Post-thin cruises are priced "per plot."[5] Assume one plot, at a cost of $18, for every three acres, meaning a per acre cost of $6.

  Then, we run the numbers.
- Scenario One: NPV of harvesting at age 25 + BLV of normal stand discounted seven years (from 25 to 18).
  - o NPV of harvesting at age 25 = $798 per acre
  - o BLV discounted seven years = $1,000/(1.06)^7 = $665
  - o Total Value = $798 + $665 = $1,463 per acre.
- Scenario Two: Cash flow of harvesting at 18 (now) + BLV of normal stand – cost of post-thin cruise
  - o Harvesting now = $500
  - o BLV of normal stand = $1,0000
  - o Per acre cost of post-thin cruise = $6
  - o Total Value = $500 + $1,000 - $6 = $1,494 per acre

If we "should have" clear cut at 18, then Scenario Two, which accounts for the cost of the post-thin cruise, will exceed Scenario One because we put the land back into its "optimal" rotation seven years sooner. The difference between One and Two provides a sense of the "lost value" from waiting and a potential "budget" for considering whether to invest in post-thin cruises regularly.

Regardless the math, there remains a qualitative aspect, a judgment call. The marginal analysis informs the decision when we have concerns by providing a tool to answer the question and support improved forest management.

---

[5] For a smaller stand of 40-acres or smaller, you might have one plot every two acres (~18-20 plots). As the stand size increases, the plot intensity decreases. For stands of 100 or 200 acres, you might have 25 plots.

Discount Rates in Forestry

Discounting future values in forestry evades simple solutions. Aside from unusually risky situations, such as high hurricane regions or unusual fire exposure, support exists for using risk-adjusted discount rates for long-term forestry projects lower than typical industrial rates. Forest economist David Klemperer (2001) emphasized how this relies on discounting true expected revenues and not on optimistic projections.

Risk occurs whenever there is a statistical distribution of potential outcomes. Think of **risk as the probability that the return of an investment will not yield what we project it will**. It reflects variation in the timing and magnitude of expected cash flows. A greater dispersion of cash flows implies greater risk.

Generally, high discount rates imply high risk and low discount rates indicate low risk (thus the term "risk adjusted"). Reductions in uncertainty can increase value in tangible ways as it allows the use of lower rates. The objective is to match appropriately a discount rate to the risk of the project (Fortson 1986).

In addition to providing context on the use and misuse of discount rates, **this section reviews approaches for estimating and adjusting discount rates for timber investments**. Questions addressed include, for example:

- How are discount rates "risk-adjusted" in forestry?
- How can discount rates get misapplied in forestry?
- How do we use WACC to estimate discount rates?
- How do we use CAPM to estimate discount rates in forestry?
- How do we adjust discount rates for inflation and taxes?

Literature Cited

Fortson, J.C. 1986. Factors affecting the discount rate for forestry investments, *Forest Products Journal* 36(6): 67-72.

Klemperer, W.D. 2001. Incorporating risk into financial analysis of forest management investments. In *Risk Analysis in Forest Management*. Kluwer Academic Publishers.

How are Discount Rates "Risk-Adjusted" in Forestry?

Answer:
Discount rates applied to forest investments can vary, depending on the property and local wood markets. However, rates tend to fall in a narrow band as analysts commonly apply three general approaches to estimating suitable rates: financial models, surveys or market evidence, and derivations from timberland transaction data.

Discussion:

Generally, **expected returns or discount rates** in forestry (or any asset class) **represent the sum of a benchmark "risk-free" rate**, such as Treasury bonds, **and a risk "premium."** Conversations about forestry discount rates can include the question, "so, how many basis points above Treasuries make sense for timberland investments?"

A technical discussion of rates may view the **risk premium** itself as **comprised of two parts: firm or asset class-specific risk (diversifiable) and market risk (affects all investments)**. For example, the Southern Pine Beatle is an asset risk specific to timber, while an economic recession takes no prisoners and affects all sectors.

Regardless, any discounted cash flow (DCF) analysis depends on specifying a valid discount rate relevant to forestry and chosen by the investor or firm. Also, credible IRRs benchmark against a rate relevant to the potential investment and chosen by the investor or firm.

Three broad approaches support estimating suitable rates in forestry:

- Derive from "first principles" or financial models. This includes the Capital Asset Pricing Model (CAPM) and the Weighted Average Cost of Capital (WACC). Financial approaches like CAPM, while useful, lost favor during the ~2007-2011 economic recession because of their dependence on benchmarks such as the S&P 500 (which performed poorly for a period of years). However, CAPM is regularly applied by finance-oriented analysts.
- Estimate based on survey evidence. Common among timberland appraisers, this includes formal and informal surveys of investors and forestry professionals, as well as evidence from real assets such as agriculture. Though less technical, surveys are practical and rely on maintaining a current understanding of timber markets and investor objectives.

- <u>Derive implied rates from transaction evidence</u>. Discount rates from actual timberland transactions provide insight into factors affecting perceived risk or attractiveness to investors. With good data, investors can match rates to different timber markets and property characteristics. This approach is the "holy grail" because it uses data from actual transactions. This is also the greatest challenge, as the details and data required make this approach elusive at best.

Guidance for Risk-Adjusting Discount Rates in Forestry

Risk-adjusting discount rates to estimate NPVs of potential forestry investments usually happens within the context of a larger firm or broader portfolio. As such, **discount rates should reflect the level of risk specific to the investment itself**, and not the risk of the overall firm. A firm should only use its own cost of capital to evaluate projects with risk profiles identical to its own.

Discount rates should reflect only the market-related, or systematic, risk of the potential investment, as we assume the balance is diversifiable within a portfolio. Systematic risk, also called "undiversifiable" risk, refers to exposures and potential losses affecting the entire market or system, such as interest rates and recessions. Unsystematic risk includes exposures specific to a firm or industry. We have little, if any, control over systematic (global) risk, while unsystematic (local) risk can be mitigated through diversification, insurance, and operational competence.

Discount rates solely relate to the risk of the investment cash flows and not the risk of any financing (i.e. bonds or loans) used to pay for the project. While financing may affect the valuation, it is not appropriate to simply discount future cash flows with the interest rate on debt used to finance the project.

Think in terms of an "investable" risk-free rate. For example, U.S. Treasuries represent a reasonable baseline opportunity cost, and you can readily deploy uninvested capital in a range of existing bonds of various durations.

Risky future cash flows are worth less than "certain" ones. For this reason, analysts spend hours building reliable growth-and-yield models for estimating future wood volumes. **Intensive forest management and trusted biological models decrease the variability of**

future harvest volumes and cash flows.[6] This reality also supports the use of lower discount rates for timberland relative to other assets.

VIEW: How Can Discount Rates Get Misapplied in Forestry?

Misapplied means to "use (something) for the wrong purpose or in the wrong way." In forest finance, we use discount rates to adjust for the risk in timber-related cash flows when conducting DCF analysis.

At times, analysts tweak discount rates qualitatively for things like the size of a project or the quality and experience of management. While a convenient form of "one stop shopping," loading the discount rate with additional criteria and obligations abuses any process focused on transparency and standardization. It reflects a misapplication.

DCF analysis provides a systematic way to organize available data and assumptions when evaluating the present value and cash flows of a going concern. The analysis does not really contemplate failure; it simply tests whether the project hits the desired financial target given the discount rate and portfolio objectives.

New York University finance professor Aswath Damodaran addressed the proper use of discount rates in a 2016 blog on valuation[7]:

> *...the discount rate exerts a pull on analysts, inviting them to use it as a receptacle for their hopes and fears. Doing so will expose you to double counting both the good stuff... and the bad...The discount rate... is meant to carry the weight of measuring going-concern risks... from the perspective of the marginal investors... That is task enough...!*

Analysts look to match discount rates to the risk of the project assuming it sits within a firm or broader portfolio. Beware practices that weaken the rigor of a given valuation. For example, understand the implications of applying discount rates that presume perfect forest operations or optimal harvest model results. While I understand the

---

[6] When teaching finance, I emphasize confirming and strengthening our understanding of potential cash flows over fine tuning the discount rate. Nailing down, to the extent possible, our expected costs and revenues better prepares us versus theorizing over discount rates.
[7] Available at: https://aswathdamodaran.blogspot.com/2016/11/myth-44-ddiscount-rate-is-receptacle.html

desire to be optimistic or forward-leaning in acquisitions, caution against the use of "perfect" cash flows and "aggressive" discount rates because, as noted by Professor Damodaran, you end up "double counting" the effects and assumptions.

Finally, discount rate selection enters treacherous waters when investors focus on what they "need" to pay to make a timberland deal happen, and then back into the discount rate, price forecast, or harvest model that plugs the valuation hole.

Discount Rates are Hurdles, Not Targets

When applying NPV to evaluate potential investments, use a discount rate that accounts for the marginal cost of capital of the firm. A company's weighted average cost of capital offers an intuitive and operable source of information for discount rates. Beating the cost of capital creates value for the firm and trailing the cost of capital destroys wealth.

If firm A raises capital at 6% and firm B finances projects at 8%, firm A has the advantage, seven days a week. They have a lower "hurdle" to jump.

The weighted average cost of capital is analogous to a credit score. If the market believes you're a credit risk, it will charge you more to borrow money.

Different firms have different risk profiles which dictate their ability to access capital. And different assets (or projects) have different risk profiles which necessitate different "discount" rates to account for the uncertainty associated with future cash flows.

Trouble begins with the fact that many firms or investors have an asset-specific discount rate in mind – their expected rate of return – rather than accounting for their cost of capital. In isolation, this does not matter much if your firm is well-capitalized and a good credit risk. But "backing into" a discount rate prioritizes the deal over the risk of the asset or the capability of the firm.

When firms apply a risk-adjusted, weighted average cost of capital for timberland investments, they contemplate the fact that any financing would occur at the cost of capital of the firm. This subjects the timberland asset to the same test any other asset would be expected to pass: given its risk profile, does it generate returns competitive to other projects or investments contemplated by the firm?

How Do We Use WACC to Estimate Discount Rates?

Answer:
We estimate the weighted average cost of capital (WACC) to quantify the cost of capital currently available to the firm or investor for both debt and equity.

Discussion and Example:

The **weighted average cost of capital (WACC) recognizes the weighted-average cost of debt-funded capital and equity capital currently available to a firm or investor**. Since capital structure and the cost of raising funds vary across firms and projects, this approach is appealing in how it can be tailored to specific investments.

Estimating WACC includes four basic steps:

1) Determine or estimate the rate of return to debt and equity holders for the firm.
2) Determine the market value and weight of the firm's debt and equity.
3) Adjust for taxes.
4) Sum the weighted returns.

The general formula for estimating WACC is the weighted average of the after-tax cost of each capital source:

$$\text{WACC} = \text{Rate}_{Debt} * (1 - \text{Tax}_{Corporate}) * \frac{\text{Debt}}{(D + E)} + \text{Rate}_{Equity} * \frac{\text{Equity}}{(D + E)}$$

Where:
Rate_{Debt} = rate of return on firm's debt
$\text{Tax}_{Corporate}$ = marginal corporate tax rate
Debt = market value of firm's debt
D + E = total market value of firm = Debt + Equity
Rate_{Equity} = expected rate of return on firm's equity
Equity = market value of firm's equity

The example below provides a range of estimates to show how WACC can be tailored to a firm's capital structure. Usually, WACC is calculated using the <u>after-tax</u> cost of each capital source. In this case, after-tax corresponds to the "WACC (corporate tax rate)."

	Lower Estimate	Middle Estimate	Upper Estimate
Cost of Equity	7.00%	9.00%	11.00%
Cost of Debt Pre-Tax	6.20%	6.65%	6.90%
Corporate Tax Rate	35.00%	35.00%	35.00%
Debt-to-value Ratio	0.4	0.3	0.25
Equity-to-value Ratio	0.6	0.7	0.75
WACC (pre-tax)	6.68%	8.30%	9.98%
WACC (corporate tax rate)	5.81%	7.60%	9.37%

When calculating WACC, use the market values for debt and equity, not the book values. Capture what it costs the firm to raise capital today. The marginal cost of debt is relatively easy to know because it approximates the current cost of debt to the firm. Mistakes are made when analysts rely on historical costs that have little relation to the financial markets' current view of the firm.

Where does the cost of equity come from? If unavailable from the client or if public firms represent our proxy, we use the capital asset pricing model (CAPM) to estimate a suitable return for equity capital.

In sum, consider three cautions when applying WACC:

- **Use market values, not book values,** for measuring firm debt-equity ratios. We want the perspective of investors, not accounting rules.
- **Ignore the firm's historical debt-equity ratio** in preference for the weights that capture the firm's preferred capital structure. We want to know what investors plan to use as their financing strategy.
- **Use the marginal tax, rather than the effective tax rate,** to reflect the taxes the firm would pay on the next dollar earned.

Situations exist when applying effective tax rates can help as clients often request this. Also, a firm may have a well-established effective tax rate that is lower than the marginal rate. In that case, applying the historic effective tax rate may be appropriate for valuation models. In practice, we apply both a client's effective and marginal tax rates when estimating a weighted average cost of capital.

How Do We Use CAPM to Estimate Discount Rates in Forestry?

Answer:

In theory, we can use the Capital Asset Pricing Model (CAPM) to estimate the required rate of return from timberland. **This assumes that**

the timber investment is being added to a well-diversified investment portfolio. However, the limited depth and availability of timber investment return data cautions the application of CAPM to forestry.

Discussion and Example:

The Capital Asset Pricing Model (CAPM) provides a method for estimating expected rates of return – the cost of equity – for financial investments and projects. CAPM relies on the principal that the market rewards investors for bearing risk; it estimates a risk "premium" that is not a function of a project's standalone risk, but rather its contribution to a diversified investment portfolio.

In other words, CAPM only considers the global, systematic risk that cannot be diversified away. Alternately, unsystematic (diversifiable) risk is specific to a company, project, or property.

Why take the position of an investor with a diversified portfolio? We assume undiversified investors perceive greater risk for a given asset than will diversified investors, who worry less about asset-specific risk. Thus, they will be willing to pay more for the asset and, over time, we would expect all assets to be held by diversified investors.

In sum, CAPM implies that the market does not reward investors for maintaining "inefficient" portfolios exposed to risks that could be eliminated through proper diversification.

The general formula for CAPM includes four variables:

$$\text{Rate} = \text{Rate}_{Free} + \text{Beta}*(\text{Rate}_{Market} - \text{Rate}_{Free})$$

Where: Rate = expected rate of return (cost of equity)
Rate_{Free} = "risk free" rate (e.g., U.S. Treasuries)
Beta = coefficient to estimate riskiness
Rate_{Market} = expected return on overall market (S&P 500)

CAPM is a linear regression equation and beta is the slope of the line. Beta is the key factor in the CAPM model. It provides a quantitative measure of the sensitivity of asset returns – in our case, timberlands – to overall market returns (e.g., S&P 500).

By definition, the overall market has a beta of 1. For betas greater than one, asset risk is higher and positively correlated with the market. Betas less than one imply risk lower than the market. The table summarizes the implications for different betas attributed to the asset.

Value of Beta	Implication
$\beta < 0$	Negative correlation; returns of asset and market move in opposite directions
$\beta = 0$	Uncorrelated returns
$0 < \beta < 1$	Returns of asset generally move in same direction, but less than, the market
$\beta = 1$	Correlated returns, both in direction and magnitude
$\beta > 1$	Returns of asset generally move in same direction, but more than, the market

The example below uses CAPM to estimate nominal and real rates. The beta comes from a previous sector analysis of the forest and paper industry. The estimated beta value of 0.91 implied that forest industry investments moved in the same direction, but less than, the overall market. For the example, CAPM implied that a suitable discount rate for a forest industry investment would be below 7% (~6.7%).

Variable	Estimate
Risk-free rate	4.00%
Beta	0.91
Overall market returns	7.00%
Estimated market premium	2.73%
Inflation Rate	2.00%
CAPM (nominal)	**6.73%**
CAPM (real)	**4.64%**

CAPM estimates the risk premium for an asset based on its relative return to the overall market. This intuitive reasoning helps explain CAPM's popularity, but it comes at a cost. **CAPM has restrictive assumptions** with respect to transaction costs (none) and information (transparent). CAPM also depends on estimates relative to a market portfolio that represents the "investable" universe. In practice, available data, context, and specific investment objectives limit the unqualified use of CAPM for estimating discount rates in forestry.

SIDEBAR: Previous Research on CAPM and Forest Investments

As noted, "CAPM is a linear regression equation and beta is the slope of the line." Beta quantifies the variability of one asset (e.g., timber) with the market (e.g., S&P 500). Investors prefer low or negative betas because they lower the risk of their portfolios.

The published literature indicates that forest asset values feature less variability than common stock portfolios because of slightly negative or close to zero correlations of timber returns relative to stock indices. In a "CAPM world," that means forestry investments have low betas that offer measurable diversification benefits.

Chris Zinkhan (1988) used CAPM to select a discount rate for long-term forestry investments by "individuals with diversified portfolios or by corporations" with diversified shareholders. Using data from 1956 through 1986, Zinkhan found a negative correlation between southern timberlands and the stock market. He concludes "southern timberland can offer a risk reduction benefit to some investors."

In 2018, Jack Lutz analyzed correlations between private timberland returns and other asset classes. He indicated it may be better to say that timberlands have limited or no correlation, especially in the case of equities. Updated analysis by Lutz in 2024 noted how public timber REITs, as tracked by the Forisk Timber REIT (FTR) Index, increasingly correlate with the S&P 500, while private timberlands remain generally uncorrelated with both the S&P 500 and FTR Index.

Literature Cited

Lutz, J. 2018. Correlation update – the heresy continues. *Forest Research Notes* Vol. 15 No. 1, 4 pages.

Lutz, J. 2024. Timber REITs and TIMOs – an update. Forest Research Notes Vol. 21 No. 2, 4 pages.

Zinkhan, F.C. 1988. Forestry projects, modern portfolio theory, and discount rate selection. *Southern Journal of Applied Forestry* 12: 132-135.

How Important is Distinguishing Real from Nominal Rates?

Years ago, a hedge fund analyst called to discuss discount rates for timberland investments. I noted, "A common error with discount rates is that folks use real and nominal rates inconsistently."

"Who cares? Mixing real and nominal is just a rounding error," responded the analyst.

Really? **Distinguishing real rates – which do not include inflation – from nominal rates – which include inflation – in forestry and timberland valuation models matters tremendously.**

While the impacts of inflation over short time periods may not matter, the effects of inflating costs and revenues over a 10-year timberland fund or 30-year forest rotation are the difference between a mountain of profits and a hole in your pocket. The error manifests when valuation models inflate costs, but not revenues, or vice versa.

Consider a simple example. Assume you paid $1,000 per acre for a five-year timberland investment with the following characteristics:

- Harvest volume: 5 tons per acre per year
- Average stumpage price, net: $20 per ton
- Taxes & administration: $10 per acre per year
- Real discount rate: 6%
- Inflation: 2%
- Nominal discount rate: 8.1%
  - 1+Nominal = (1+Real)(1+Inflation)=(1.06)*(1.02)

After 5-years, we sell the property for $1,000 per acre in real terms [e.g., we sold the dirt for the same price we paid in today's dollars]. The table shows the range of potential NPVs resulting from mixing real and nominal revenues and costs, in addition to discounting annual net cash flows ("net income") with real versus nominal rates.

Net Present Value (NPV) Calculations

Net Income Calculation		Discount Rate	
Revenues	Costs	Real	Nominal
Real	Real	$126.37	$35.03
Real	Nominal	$123.88	$32.70
Nominal	Nominal	$226.58	$126.37
Nominal	Real	$229.07	$128.69

Note that using real revenues, real costs, and a real discount rate produces an NPV of $126.37, which is identical to using nominal revenues, nominal costs, and a nominal discount rate. **The key is consistency**.

Inflation must be considered – or explicitly set aside – when evaluating long-term investments such as timberlands. Otherwise, results can distort or mislead.

When given the option, I prefer conducting comparative analysis in nominal terms. Why? Financial statements and timber price services tend to capture and report in nominal terms. Also, the returns of most non-forestry assets are reported in nominal terms, so it simplifies benchmarking and comparisons with other asset classes.

How Do We Adjust Discount Rates for Inflation and Taxes?

Answer:

Follow the process detailed by Steven Bullard and John Gunter in their 2000 article on this topic (or ask someone else to do it or use the Excel "discount rate adjustor" in the *Applied Forest Finance* course materials).

Discussion and Example:

A common error in DCF analysis associated with forestry investments is failing to account for taxes and inflation. One example is applying a before-tax discount rate to after-tax costs and revenues. Another is comparing forestry investment returns with today's (uninflated) timber prices to bonds stated in nominal (inflated) terms.

Usually, investors and firms specify the discount rate or cost of capital in advance. If DCF analysis is conducted on an after-tax basis, an after-tax discount rate should be used. As noted, **the key is consistency**.

In 2000, Steven Bullard and John Gunter published an article in the *Southern Journal of Applied Forestry* ("Adjusting Discount Rates for Income Taxes and Inflation") that provided a step-by-step process for adjusting rates in this case. I summarize their approach here.

Step 1: Using the grid below, find the quadrant for the current discount rate (the discount rate that you have in hand).

Step 2: Using the grid, find the quadrant for the discount rate that you need (the discount rate that you want to calculate).

	Before Taxes	After Taxes
Nominal (inflated)	Quadrant 1: Nominal rate, before taxes	Quadrant 2: Nominal rate, after taxes
Real (no inflation)	Quadrant 3: Real rate, before taxes	Quadrant 4: Real rate, after taxes

Step 3: Using the relevant tax rate and/or inflation assumption, apply the proper formula from the table below to adjust the discount rate. For investors, the tax rate is their marginal income tax rate.

Quadrant	Type of Rate Adjustment
1) 1 → 2	Nominal, before tax to after tax
2) 2 → 1	Nominal, after tax to before tax
3) 1 → 3	Before tax, nominal to real
4) 3 → 1	Before tax, real to nominal
5) 2 → 4	After tax, nominal to real
6) 4 → 2	After tax, real to nominal
7) 3 → 4	Real, before tax to after tax
8) 4 → 3	Real, after tax to before tax

Quadrant	Formula Required to Make Adjustment
1) 1 → 2	After tax = before tax * (1 - income tax rate)
2) 2 → 1	Before tax = after tax/(1 - income tax rate)
3) 1 → 3	Real before tax = (1 + nominal before tax)/(1 + inflation rate) - 1
4) 3 → 1	Nominal before tax = real before tax + inflation + real before tax*inflation
5) 2 → 4	Real after tax = (1 + nominal after tax)/(1 + inflation rate) - 1
6) 4 → 2	Nominal after tax = real after tax + inflation + real after tax*inflation
7) 3 → 4	Reat after tax = real before tax*(1 - income tax rate) - [income tax rate*inflation/(1 + inflation)]
8) 4 → 3	Real before tax = real after tax/(1 - inc. tax rate) + inc. tax rate/(1 - inc. tax rate)*[inflation/(1-inflation)]

As an example, a forest investment has an 8.2% real, after-tax return. Will this attract your client, who has a hurdle rate of 10% real before taxes? To answer, we adjust the client's real rate from a before-tax to an after-tax basis. Assume a marginal income tax rate of 28% and expected inflation of 3%.

Step 1: our current real, before tax rate is in Quadrant 3.
Step 2: our desired real, after-tax discount rate is in Quadrant 4.
Step 3: going from 3 to 4 is formula 7.

Real after tax = 10%*(1-28%) − [28%*3%/(1+3%)]
= 6.4%

The client's 10% real before tax discount rate is equivalent to a 6.4% real after tax discount rate assuming a 28% tax rate and 3% inflation. Therefore, yes, our forestry investment with the 8.2% real after tax return looks attractive, as it exceeds 6.4%.

Discount Rates in Low-Interest Rate Environments

After the financial crisis of 2007-2008, the U.S. economy experienced years of low interest rates, which encouraged borrowing by firms and justified low discount rates in DCF models across industries, including timberland. One observation from this period is how the application of low discount rates extends the relevance of (environmental) risks and disruptions occurring far into the future.

Think of the math at play. Discounting $1,000 received in 50 years at 10% delivers $8.52 in present value, barely enough for a burger and fries. Discount that same $1,000 in 50 years at 1.43% (the yield on 30-year U.S. Treasuries as of July 1, 2020) equals $491.68.

At 10%, disruptions in 30 or 40 years have little impact on the analysis in terms of value today. At 1.43%, events in 30 or 40 years materially affect present value. The reduced impact of time on value from low discount rates creates an analytic tradeoff, turning once marginal projects into viable ones, even if nothing else changed in the assessment of the asset (or the local wood markets).

How, as analysts, do we contemplate these issues in our work? If rates are "historically" or "unsustainably" low, we can account for this with the risk premiums, as the signal from the low interest rate provides its own indication of concern about the economy. One place to look for guidance on the increment is the actual borrowing costs for firms in the forest products industries relative to treasuries.

Ultimately, we want the timberland valuation and wood market analysis to stand on the merits of their (1) bottom-up facts and (2) top-down attractiveness relative to other assets. The discount rate, in this view, is baselined to the long-term cyclical risk of the industry first and then adjusted for the specifics of the local asset and market.

Sensitivity Analysis

Sensitivity analysis provides a way to test the relative importance of inputs and assumptions to the performance of potential investments. In forest finance, it can clarify our understanding of relationships between management costs, timber prices, discount rates, and other localized forest factors given available data and our analysis.

This section reviews, with examples, sensitivity analysis when analyzing forestry investments and valuing timberlands.

When Should We Conduct Sensitivity Analysis?

Sensitivity analysis clarifies factors that drive or threaten investment performance; the inability to point these out indicates a lack of preparation or transparency. The practice tests inputs in an orderly, systematic way. Modifying key variables, one at a time, helps demonstrate their relative importance to NPV, IRR, or other criteria.

Situations for conducting sensitivity analysis include:

1. Uncertainty associated with key variables and assumptions applied in the analysis,
2. Results that barely qualify based on the accept/reject criterion.

In short, if you're worried about an input, or your project barely qualifies, apply sensitivity analysis.

Timberland returns largely depend on three things. One, what you pay for the forest. Two, how long you stay invested. Three, how much you pay in fees to manage everything. Returns in forestry are highly sensitive to discount rates, realized sawtimber volumes, and sawtimber prices. Sensitivity analysis supports the testing and ranking of these factors to better manage risk and optimize returns.

EXAMPLE: How Sensitive are Forestland Values to Changes in Management Costs and Timber Prices?

Answer:

Intensive forest management increases financial returns for softwood stands through more volume, shorter rotations, and increased percentages of higher valued sawtimber and chip-n-saw. Forest investments can endure large swings in management costs and prices of lower grade products and still perform; however, forest ROIs are highly sensitive to discount rates, realized sawtimber volumes, and sawtimber prices.

Discussion and example:

In the Q1 2018 *Forisk Research Quarterly*, Forisk analyzed the sensitivity of forestland values to changes in reforestation costs, timber prices and management intensity. Estimating the return on investment (ROI) from active forest management requires comparing different management strategies in terms of costs and volume gains by product.

We outlined two forest management plans for a typical Piedmont site in the U.S. South. "Basic" is a simple plant-thin-harvest strategy, while "Intensive" includes additional silviculture investments.

Forest Management Regimes and Key Cost Assumptions[8]

Plan Summaries	Basic	Intensive
Thinnings	Once	Twice
Competition control	No	Yes
Fertilization	No	Twice
Site prep & plant	$200	$200
Fertilize at planting		$100
Competition control		$35
Fertilize mid-rotation		$120
Total Costs	**$200**	**$455**

Pine forests in the U.S. South generate higher volumes when owners invest in site-appropriate treatments that enhance tree regeneration (site preparation); improve seedlings (genetics); address nutrient deficiencies (fertilization); and reduce competition for nutrients from weeds or hardwoods. These activities can increase incremental volumes by 10% to 60+%.

Applying two forest management regimes to high quality sites produced distinct results. The "Basic" plan grew 140 tons/acre over a 26-year rotation while the "Intensive" plan produced 195 tons/acre (39% more) over a 24-year rotation. While lower-valued pulpwood accounted for 57% of the "Basic" production, the highest valued sawtimber accounted for 46% of the "Intensive" volume.

---

[8] "Basic" approximates a 60 site index (SI); "Intensive" exhibits an effective SI of 80; both assume $8/acre/year of admin/property tax expenses.

Production by Product and Bare Land Values (BLV) for Each Regime

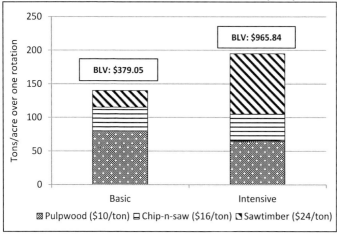

Note: 5% real discount rate

Though intensive forest management increases costs, it materially increases financial returns through more volume, shorter rotations, and higher percentages of more valuable logs. Based on BLV, the Intensive plan creates nearly $600 per acre of additional value (+155%) to the forest owner.

Sensitivity Analysis of BLV, +/-10% for Key Inputs for Intensive Plan

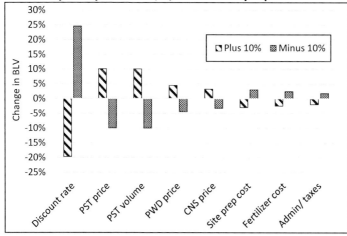

Sensitivity analysis indicates that higher BLVs from intensive management persist against higher silviculture costs. In testing the sensitivity of per acre BLVs versus 10% increases or decreases in key variables, the estimated financial returns can endure large swings in management costs, and volumes or prices of lower grade products. However, forest management ROIs are highly sensitive to discount rates, realized sawtimber volumes, and sawtimber prices.

EXAMPLE: Testing Discount Rates

Numbers outperform words when clarifying the sensitivity of timberland values to discount rates. Assume a forest requires investments totaling $235 per acre by year one and generates per acre cash flows of $1,000 in 15 years and $2,400 in 25 years. As the discount rate increases, the NPV falls from the undiscounted $3,165 ($2,400 + $1,000 - $45 - $190) per acre at 0% to $434 per acre with cash flows discounted at 8%.

Net Present Value (NPV) at Different Discount Rates

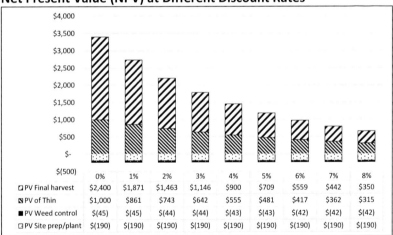

	0%	1%	2%	3%	4%	5%	6%	7%	8%
▨ PV Final harvest	$2,400	$1,871	$1,463	$1,146	$900	$709	$559	$442	$350
▨ PV of Thin	$1,000	$861	$743	$642	$555	$481	$417	$362	$315
■ PV Weed control	$(45)	$(45)	$(44)	$(44)	$(43)	$(43)	$(42)	$(42)	$(42)
▢ PV Site prep/plant	$(190)	$(190)	$(190)	$(190)	$(190)	$(190)	$(190)	$(190)	$(190)

Consider the implications for valuations. Discounting the $2,400 final harvest revenue generated in 25 years at 2% yields $1,463 in present value, a total discount of 39%. Using 4% yields $900 (a discount of 62%) and using 8% yields $350 (85%). The long time periods often required for a forest's biggest cash flows magnify the sensitivity of timberland valuations to discount rates.

Debt and Taxes

Debt and taxes affect forestry investment returns. The use of leverage (debt) can reduce the need for cash when acquiring timberland properties and increase returns on investment, but it can also affect flexibility with available cash in the future. Tax policy, which can impact net returns to forest owners, also provides mechanisms to recover and redistribute forestry investments made over time. These mechanisms generally encourage forest management and reinvestment by private landowners.

This section introduces key debt and tax concepts, along with requirements and strategies relevant to timberland investments and forestland owners.

What are Key Tax Issues for Forest Landowners?

Taxes matter. **Ultimately, investors care about after-tax cash flows and values.** Once income is withheld or designated for taxes, it is unavailable for consumption or investment. Forest landowners and timberland investors are subject to local and federal taxes, and these differ by state and county (and country).

Reference materials on taxes for forest landowners are available from the USDA Forest Service. Here I summarize key points from bulletins published on the National Timber Tax Website to assist forest landowners in preparing their individual tax returns (current as of January 2024). To read the complete, current USFS bulletin, go to www.timbertax.org.

- Specify the nature of your forest ownership each tax year. Tax rules vary by your designation of the forest for personal use, investment, or business.
- Know your timber basis. Timber basis comprises the total sum you paid for and spent on acquiring the property. This includes legal, accounting, survey and other fees directly related to due diligence and closing on the timber property. Basis also becomes directly relevant with inherited timberlands.
- Understand timber depletion. Depletion, like depreciation and amortization, is a cost recovery method for natural resources. It comprises the costs we have in the timber we own and harvest. We

subtract depletion from timber revenues to arrive at taxable income. Ultimately, we want to minimize taxes paid within the guidelines set forth by the IRS. (More on depletion later.)

- <u>Casualty and theft losses matter.</u> Unexpected timber losses resulting from natural catastrophes or events such as storm damage, fires, or theft may provide tax deductions. Details for capturing these deductions are specified by the IRS and often require a third-party appraisal.
- <u>File Form T.</u> Form T is the "Forest Activities Schedule." Filing is required to claim timber depletion deductions or to sell timber in situations relevant to Sections 631(a) or 631(b).

Other issues relevant to forest ownership include exposure to the net investment income tax (NIIT), the receipt of form 1099-S after certain timber sales (corporate and larger businesses are exempt), and details related to like-kind exchanges and potential cost-sharing programs.

Avoiding taxes is legal and encouraged, but evading taxes is illegal. The most important way to secure full benefits under the IRS: maintain good records of revenues and expenses.

KEY CONCEPT: What is Timber "Depletion"?

After investing funds to plant trees, forest owners often wait decades before receiving the associated harvest revenues. This gap in time affects the matching of expenses to revenues, accounting for taxable income, and reporting of earnings.

Depletion represents the costs we have in the timber we own and harvest. Like depreciation and amortization, it is a cost recovery method. Without depletion to account for the "cost" of timber sold, a forest owner would basically get taxed on gross revenue.

Depletion is one of several non-cash items that must be accounted for when calculating after-tax cash flows. **We subtract depletion from timber stumpage revenues to arrive at taxable income. Therefore, we want depletion rates as high as possible!**

There are two general methods for calculating depletion: tax depletion and financial depletion. **Tax depletion** is based on the actual cost of the timber, adjusted annually for additions (acquisitions), removals (harvests), annual net growth, and capitalized reforestation costs. The depletion "rate" or "unit" for a corporation is capitalized silviculture dollars divided by the merchantable forest inventory.

Financial depletion, also called "normalized" depletion, sums all capitalized silviculture expenses plus merchantable timber accounts and divides this by the beginning inventory plus all growth over the rotation. In concept, this should represent the initial cost of the timber plus all ongoing capitalized silviculture expenditures and all the wood that is grown. This approach provides an "average rate" over the rotation rather than a rate that can change drastically over one rotation. You often find this method in financial reporting by public firms.

In summary, depletion reduces the taxes we pay on revenues produced from harvesting and marketing timber. We deduct depletion from net timber sale proceeds. Public firms generally report both tax depletion and financial depletion. Ultimately, the objective is to minimize taxes paid within IRS guidelines.

EXAMPLE: How Do I Evaluate the Use of Leverage in a Timberland Investment?

Answer:
Understand the lender's perspective: at the end of the day, can the investment, and investor (you), service the debt and pay the bills?

Discussion and Example:
In October 2009, *The Economist* magazine, in "The Nature of Wealth," noted, "those who buy an overvalued asset with borrowed money have not made themselves richer but poorer." This quote captures both an important idea and overstated concern with respect to timberland investments. **The important idea: know what you're buying to avoid overpaying. The overstated concern: avoid leverage (debt).** In practice, **there are entirely practical and appropriate applications for debt** in forestry investments.

For starters, **the U.S. tax code favors debt** over other sources of external financing. Interest payments on debt are tax deductible as expenses. This alone merits "looking under the hood" at the issue.

A lesson with debt financing has been that successful investors have specific, measured, and time-based objectives for their timberland investments and overall portfolios. Jason Denton, a friend and forester with deep experience providing debt financing to timber investors, helped me outline situations for considering leverage in forestry:

1. Investors simply need capital to make investments. The timberland property costs $1 million; you have $500,000. Borrowing provides one way to close the gap (and the transaction).
2. Investors want to preserve and extend capital. A forested property costs $1 million; you have $1 million. However, you want to retain "dry powder" to pursue other investments. Rather than use all available funds for this investment, you borrow to preserve capital for operating costs or other deals.
3. Investors need liquidity. In cases, an investor already owns a timber property that may or may not use leverage. Due to irregular cash flows – a normal situation for timberland assets – the investor may need supplementary funds between periodic cash flows.
4. Investors want to boost their return on equity (ROE). A common investment objective with real estate, it also applies, in cases, for timberland investors looking to increase returns. Consider an example across a range of debt levels for a $1 million acquisition and the relative impacts on ROE.

	No Leverage	10% Leverage	25% Leverage	40% Leverage
Total Investment	$1,000,000	$1,000,000	$1,000,000	$1,000,000
Annual Income	$60,000	$60,000	$60,000	$60,000
Interest Rate	5.0%	5.0%	5.0%	5.0%
Borrowed Funds	$0	$100,000	$250,000	$400,000
Annual Interest	$0	$5,000	$12,500	$20,000
Net Income	$60,000	$55,000	$47,500	$40,000
Equity Invested	$1,000,000	$900,000	$750,000	$600,000
Return on Equity (ROE)	6.0%	6.1%	6.3%	6.7%

The example above does not account for appreciation or depreciation in asset values. Consider the no leverage and 25% leverage cases with 5% appreciation and 5% depreciation scenarios in values. The table below shows the relative ROE impacts when asset values change.[9]

---

[9] Note that the example does not account for the ability to net annual interest expense against ordinary taxable while, while revenues from timber get taxed at capital gains rates. The implications of this varies across investors.

78

	No Leverage	No Leverage	25% Leverage	25% Leverage
Total Investment	$1,000,000	$1,000,000	$1,000,000	$1,000,000
Annual Income	$60,000	$60,000	$60,000	$60,000
Interest Rate	5.0%	5.0%	5.0%	5.0%
Borrowed Funds	$0	$0	$250,000	$250,000
Annual Interest	$0	$0	$12,500	$12,500
Net Income	$60,000	$60,000	$47,500	$47,500
Equity Invested	$1,000,000	$1,000,000	$750,000	$750,000
Change in Asset Value	$50,000	($50,000)	$50,000	($50,000)
Value of Invested Equity	$1,050,000	$950,000	$800,000	$700,000
Return on Equity (ROE)	*11.0%*	*1.0%*	*13.0%*	*-0.3%*

With no leverage, investors earn returns in proportion to total timberland returns. For example, $60,000 in income plus $50,000 of asset appreciation equals a total gain of $110,000 on a $1,000,0000 investment for an ROE of 11%. A $50,000 reduction in asset value leads to an ROE of 1%. **Leverage increases the investors' exposure to the gains, and losses, in asset values, generating higher and lower ROEs.**

Timberland investors and timber-owning corporations have other reasons for using debt. These include (1) the desire to finance a distribution from an unleveraged asset (especially in a low-interest rate environment when a cash payout may be desirable), or (2) extending the life of a mature timberland fund, where the manager would rather extend than reduce returns by forcing a sale in a depressed market.

When Does Leverage Make Sense for Timberland Investments?

Leverage works well for tracts with suitable product and age class distributions. It can be harder to justify loans on pre-merchantable stands with no potential for near-term cash flows.

From the lender's perspective**, the most critical aspect of underwriting a loan is the cash flow analysis**. This should also be the most important consideration for you as the borrower. In short, can the investment – and investor (you) – service the debt and pay the bills?

The true measure of **servicing debt depends on the ability of the timberland asset to generate and sustain annual cash flows in amounts required to easily meet the annual debt payments.** Why focus on cash flows and not on profitability? Because borrowers can "camouflage" profits (net income) with non-cash expenses such as depreciation, depletion, and amortization.

The standard measure for assessing how easily an investor can pay interest on outstanding debt is the **"coverage ratio."** It is calculated each year by dividing net cash flow (or EBITDA[10]) by the interest expense for the same period. Lenders prefer coverage ratios greater than one.

How do Investors Finance Timberland?

Investors typically work with institutional and regional lenders familiar with the cash flow patterns of timberland assets. For certain financiers, financing timberland represents a lower-risk activity in a long-term, asset class. Well-managed, diversified timberland properties in strong wood markets generate solid cash flows backed by durable, reliable collateral.

Financial institutions serving the timberland sector typically have specialized forestry experience and expertise. This helps them evaluate lending opportunities given the needs and objectives of the borrower, and the expected cash flow cycle of the timberland property. Lenders prioritize the creditworthiness of the borrower and the quality of the asset, which serves as the collateral.

For larger timberland transactions requiring tens or hundreds of millions of dollars, insurance firms and Farm Credit banks often partner to "service the deal." Anecdotally, **loan-to-values (LTVs), on average, fall in the 25-40% range, while many investors use no debt**.

Loan-to-value means you know the loan amount and the asset value. When folks apply debt, they create a situation that must, ultimately, be unwound, so we want to be sensitive to this as the exposure extends beyond the asset and to the firm.

Timberland loans can be structured with fixed or variable rates. A benefit of fixed-rate loans is the convenience and certainty of a fixed loan structure with known payments. Variable rate loans may prove more attractive for assets with mature, harvestable forest inventories.

Pre-payment terms can vary between fixed-rate and variable-rate loans. A lender might charge a premium or fee to allow borrowers to pre-pay principal on a fixed-rate loan. Alternately, variable rate loans typically allow the borrower to pay down principal along the way and/or when the rate is reset.

---

[10] Earnings before interest, taxes, depreciation, and amortization.

Timberland Investing, Investments, and Benchmarks

Timberland assets, like bonds, provide a way to preserve wealth and store value. They offer a safe-haven and portfolio diversifier for a range of investors. Many investors rely on experienced professionals to provide forest management services and access to timber markets.

Timberland values, like those of commercial real estate and farmland, derive from their ability to generate income. As a real asset capable of growing raw material for fuel and the manufacture of forest products, timberland readily generates cash flow for its owners. The composition of these flows is of great import and interest.

Three general approaches exist for investing in forests and timberlands. First, invest directly through buying, owning, and managing forests and land. Second, place funds with an intermediary, an asset manager, to acquire and manage timberland investments on your behalf. Third, buy shares (equity) of public firms that own timberland and generate most of their income from growing and selling timber.

This section introduces the nature, history, and structure of common timberland investment vehicles, and outlines methods for benchmarking their financial performance.

Owning Timberlands Means Buying into an Operating Business

Direct timberland investing means buying into an operating business that grows and supplies raw material to wood-using manufacturers located within economically viable distances of the forest. It also provides supplementary income opportunities from recreational leases, cell phone towers, forest carbon, real estate, and other ventures.

Investors sometimes ask, "Why do market values for this forest differ from what we estimated with our models?" Ranges in returns are partly attributable to variances in management and execution, as well as differences in local and end markets affecting a given property.

Land value is a function of its ability to generate income. In cases, non-timber land uses have higher returns, or the estimated timber returns for one investor differ from another, given variances in assumed yields, timber prices, costs, and discount rates.

While discussing forest management, a retired client told me, "Use strategies that maximize the volume of trees of reasonable quality at minimum cost and assume that technology will create the value." This advice has held up well.

Investors hold timberlands for reasons that are largely diversifying and defensive. Value is created over time through multiple sources, and to the extent we put arbitrary 5 or 10-year time horizons on the asset, we constrain performance and change our exposures to the associated risks. As investments, forest assets are resilient operating enterprises. Understanding and managing time is a strategic part of this.

Traditional Drivers of Timberland Returns

When investing in timberland, the price paid crucially affects the ultimate profitability. Outside of acquisition price, timberland investment returns are largely a function of (1) biological tree growth; (2) timber price changes; and (3) land value appreciation. The extent to which each drives returns depends on the specific tract location relative to wood-using mills and population centers. **Location matters.**

Biological growth, which includes (1) increases in volume and weight and (2) enhanced value from a lower-valued tree growing into a higher-priced one, remains a core element of the timber investment calculus. It offers the most basic form of "optionality" as larger diameter trees can be used for a wider range of mostly higher-valued end products.

Active forest investment management includes leveraging all available cash flows from recreation and hunting to newer markets such as carbon sequestration and solar energy. Increasing forest productivity occurs through investments in improved seedlings and a range of intensive silvicultural treatments. Productive forests support higher cash flows and values.

Land gets more valuable when you plant it and put it to work. Timberland returns increase when improved with NPV-positive projects. Enhanced forest management, better roads, and new leases get reflected in present value. The prospects for harvesting trees during poor weather by improving the roads instantly increases the value of your forest over the neighbor's, all other things being equal.

Trees have certain characteristics. To manage timber stands well, the forest manager must understand how trees grow and react to changes in the local environment to increase timber production. In the end, **anything that increases present value faster than the investor's opportunity cost enhances value.** So, please take the easy wins.

SIDEBAR: Framework for Forest Carbon

A happy consequence of forest growth is the absorption of CO_2 from the atmosphere. Markets compensating forest owners for the carbon sequestered by their trees attempt to match a low-cost "supply" of greenhouse gas (GHG) emissions mitigation with demand for offsetting credits. Forest carbon could augment timberland values to the extent that markets for carbon support reliable cash flows.

Forest carbon offset projects include three key approaches:

- Afforestation (planting or replanting trees);
- Avoided conversion (keeping forests as forests); and
- Improved forest management (IFM) to increase sequestration.

Anything that affects forest growth, forest cover, or forest health affects carbon sequestration, as considered by these projects.

Forest owners must compare the traditional selling of timber to local mills with diverting harvests to sell carbon credits. The framework below shows the tradeoffs, which vary across timber markets.

Framework to Assess Forest Carbon Potential in Local Markets

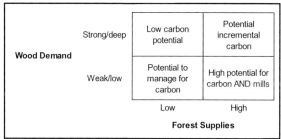

For markets with strong wood demand, expect less impact from carbon. In markets with abundant forest supplies and fewer mills, forest carbon programs provide incentives to retain land in trees. In sum, we look for timberland owners to match strategies to local markets.

Comparing Timberland Investment Vehicles

Investors have three basic ways to add timberland to their portfolios, not including those available through debt markets (e.g. making loans or buying bonds in timberland-owning companies).

First, investors can directly acquire and manage timberlands. With this, investors enjoy the full diversification, wealth preservation, and cash flow benefits of owning trees. Ownership also requires the capital and ongoing commitment of hiring and maintaining the forestry and operational expertise required to manage the assets.

Second, investors can outsource by providing funds to a timberland investment specialist to acquire and manage timberland assets on their behalf. Institutional investors, for example, will work with a timberland investment management organization (TIMO). With TIMOs, investors have options, from employing a single-investor separate account to participating in a commingled fund with other investors to joining a "fund-of-funds" that pools capital for use in a set of commingled funds managed by different TIMOs.

Third, investors can "go public" and acquire shares in traded timberland-owning real estate investment trusts (timber REITs). This is the most liquid of the three investment approaches.

Tell Me More About TIMOs and REITs

TIMOs (timberland investment management organizations) and REITs (real estate investment trusts) provide two ways to invest in timber. TIMOs are asset managers that serve, primarily, family offices and institutional investors. REITs provide a tax efficient, liquid vehicle for individual investors and institutions.

TIMOs are intermediaries between investors and their timberland assets. TIMOs themselves do not own timberland; they buy, manage, and sell land and timber on behalf of their clients, including institutional investors such as banks, foundations, pension funds and endowments, as well as individuals and family offices.

In the United States as of 2024, approximately 20 TIMOs managed nearly 19 million acres on behalf of investors. According to Forisk's 2024 Timberland Owner & Manager List, the largest U.S. TIMOs included Manulife (formerly Hancock; 3.4 million acres in the U.S.); Resource Management Service (2.1 million acres); and Forest Investment Associates (1.8 million acres).

REITs own and manage income producing real estate such as buildings, warehouses, rental properties, and, since 1999, timberlands. As of 2024, the public timber REITs included Weyerhaeuser (10.5 million acres), Rayonier (2.3 million acres), and PotlatchDeltic (2.2 million).

To qualify as a REIT under IRS rules, a firm must satisfy specific criteria, the most important of which to shareholders is the requirement to distribute annually at least 90% of its taxable income in the form of dividends. Unlike C-corporations, REITs may deduct the dividends they pay to shareholders from taxable income. As such, REITs address "double taxation," where a firm pays income taxes and shareholders also pay taxes on the after-tax income distributed as dividends. With REITs, shareholders pay taxes on dividends received, but firms do not pay taxes on income generated from real estate.

How did Institutional Timberland Investing Develop in the U.S.?

Summary:
Between 1960 and 1999, new legislation, tax policy, and corporate mergers drove changes to industrial timberland ownership, shifting forests from integrated firms to institutions and timber specialists.

Discussion:
In 1969, 14 of the 15 largest US timberland owners were vertically integrated, mill-owning forest industry firms; as of 2024, only two of the top timberland owners from 1969 still held places on the list. Years ago, integrated forest industry firms dominated the industry; today, timberland specialists (e.g. REITs) and asset managers (e.g. TIMOs) control the largest investment-grade forests. What happened?

Institutional timberland investing in the U.S. evolved from mundane yet structurally powerful legislative changes.[11] In 1960, President Dwight Eisenhower signed a collection of unrelated tax laws known as the Cigar Excise Tax Extension of 1960. This bill included the Real Estate Investment Trust Act of 1960. REITs are companies that own and manage income-producing real estate of various types, such as office buildings, warehouses, and timberlands.

---

[11] Mendell, B.C. 2016. From Cigar Tax to Timberland Trusts: A Short History of Timber REITs and TIMOs, *Forest History Today*, Spring/Fall 2016: 32-36.

Top 15 Industrial U.S. Timberland Owners & Managers, 1969 vs 2024

Rank	1969		2024	
	Firm	Type	Firm	Type
1	International Paper	Forest Industry	Weyerhaeuser	Public REIT
2	Weyerhaeuser	Forest Industry	Manulife (Hancock)	TIMO
3	Georgia-Pacific	Forest Industry	Sierra Pacific Industries	Forest Industry
4	Great Northern Nekoosa	Forest Industry	Rayonier	Public REIT
5	St. Regis Paper	Forest Industry	Green Diamond Resource Company	Private
6	Boise Cascade	Forest Industry	The Nature Conservancy	Conservation
7	Scott Paper	Forest Industry	PotlatchDeltic	Public REIT
8	Champion International	Forest Industry	Resource Management Service (RMS)	TIMO
9	Kimberly-Clark	Forest Industry	Forest Investment Associates (FIA)	TIMO
10	Burlington Northern	Railroad	Molpus Woodlands Group	TIMO
11	Union Camp	Forest Industry	Aurora Sustainable Lands	Private
12	Continental Group	Forest Industry	BTG Pactual	TIMO
13	Crown Zellerbach	Forest Industry	Lyme Timber Company	TIMO
14	Potlatch	Forest Industry	J.D. Irving	Forest Industry
15	Diamond International	Forest Industry	Tall Timbers Trust	Private

Sources: Forisk 2024 Timberland Owner & Manager List; Enk 1974

In the 1970s, U.S. industrial timberland started to shift from vertically integrated firms that owned sawmills and paper plants to forestry specialists. Part of this resulted from an economic disconnect. In 1978, Goldman Sachs analyst Thomas Clephane dissected the forest ownerships in the forest products industry. His work indicated that the stock prices of most of the largest forest products companies were trading below the value of their timberlands.

This gap in value between the timberlands and shares of certain firms provided opportunities. The forest industry began selling their forests prior to the recession of 1981 and 1982, and the subsequent cash from these sales balanced broader forest industry struggles. Firms were closing mills, laying off workers, and writing off hundreds of millions of dollars. The divestiture of timberlands accelerated.

Timberland sellers found interest from institutions looking to diversify their pension plans. The Employee Retirement Income Security Act of 1974 (ERISA) triggered a change in how pension funds invested. Congress designed ERISA to regulate private pension plans, requiring them to diversify beyond bonds and stocks. Timberland, with its regular cash flows and potential to hedge inflation, became a viable alternative.

TIMOs stepped in to support these transactions. Institutions placed funds with the TIMOs as their intermediaries, and the TIMOs acquired and managed timberland investments on their behalf.

Timber REITs arrived in 1999, beginning with the conversion of Plum Creek from a master limited partnership to a REIT. Between 1999 and 2006, four public forest products firms owning more than 12 million acres of industrial timberlands became REITs. In addition to Plum Creek, these included Rayonier, Potlatch, and briefly, Longview Fibre.

In 2010, Weyerhaeuser converted to a REIT. In 2013, CatchMark Timber Trust, formerly the private REIT known as Wells Timber, became the sixth timber REIT to trade publicly. In February 2016, Plum Creek merged into Weyerhaeuser. The new firm held over 13 million acres at the time across 20 states (and Uruguay). In 2022, CatchMark Timber Trust merged into PotlatchDeltic (formerly Potlatch).

How did Investors Respond to Timber REITs?

In 2008, Forisk researchers completed the first peer-reviewed study of public timber REITs.[12] We analyzed stock market responses to four announcements of forest industry firms converting from traditional C-corporations to real estate investment trusts. The announcements were Plum Creek in 1998, Rayonier in 2003, Potlatch in 2005, and Longview Fiber in 2005.

Cumulative Abnormal Returns for Firms Becoming Public Timber REITs

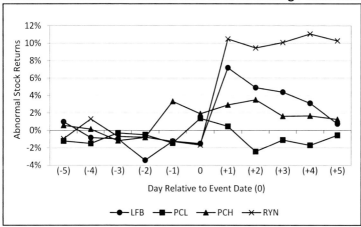

All four announcements were associated with significant abnormal increases in the stock prices of the four firms on the day before, day of, or day after each firm's announced REIT conversion (see figure). Results confirmed investor preferences for holding timberlands within a REIT rather than a traditional C-corporation structure.

---

[12] Mendell, B.C., N. Mishra, and T. Sydor. 2008. Investor Responses to Timberlands Structured as Real Estate Investment Trusts (REITs), *Journal of Forestry*, 106(5): 277-280.

DISCUSSION: How Should You Apply the NCREIF Timberland Index When Evaluating Performance?

Answer:

When using the NCREIF Timberland Index for benchmarking purposes, (1) use the annualized returns; (2) prioritize NCREIF as a national, rather than regional, benchmark; (3) avoid NCREIF as a standalone measure of timberland manager performance; and (4) use weighted averages of the regional indices to better approximate your actual portfolio.

Discussion:

      For alternative investments (such as timberlands), benchmarks often serve as incomplete indicators, a challenge described in a 2014 *The Wall Street Journal* article ("Benchmarking Alternative Funds an Inexact Science"). Alternative-fund benchmarks function well as a "guidepost" but not as true metrics for individual investments. This can prove problematic for institutions seeking guidance when making investment decisions and evaluating asset managers.

      The National Council of Real Estate Investment Fiduciaries (NCREIF) publishes widely referenced indices for private U.S. timberland investments managed by TIMOs on behalf of institutions. In "Best Practices and Existing Indices for Privately Held Timber Assets" (Q3 2015 *Forisk Research Quarterly*), Forisk detailed seven criteria for evaluating timberland indices such as NCREIF. Applying the benchmark criteria to NCREIF's Timberland Index resulted in four recommendations for the maximal use of NCREIF without abusing its capabilities.

1. <u>Use annualized returns for benchmarking purposes</u>. NCREIF reports timberland investment results quarterly. However, the lagging associated with appraisal-based real estate indices (such as NCREIF) generally question the use of quarterly returns for performance analysis. Rather, annual appreciation and income measures have proved useful, helpful, and robust for timberland tracking.

2. <u>Use NCREIF primarily as a U.S. national benchmark; avoid using regional measures outside of the South or Northwest</u>. NCREIF reports investment returns in four U.S. regions: South, Northwest, Lake States, and Northeast. However, NCREIF's tracking is heavily weighted to the South and, to a lesser extent, the Northwest.

3. <u>Avoid using NCREIF returns as a stand-alone measure of timberland manager performance</u>. NCREIF does a better job of summarizing returns through economic cycles from timberlands than it does of

comparing manager skills, strategies, or effectiveness. We suggest supplementing NCREIF with assessments of communication skills and annual variance analysis of pro-forma budgets. This could include benchmarking management costs. The bottom line: "does your manager (or lawyer, accountant, etc.) do what they said they were going to do when they said they were going to do it? Do they communicate this well?" Also, clarify the day-to-day realities of what the manager accomplished on your behalf while dealing with exogenous factors outside of their control.

Annual Compounded Rates of Return for Timberland Investments

Asset Class	Index	2000-2010	2006-2016	Notes
Private Timberlands	US Total (NCREIF)	6.82%	5.83%	A
Private Timberlands	US South (NCREIF)	6.69%	5.07%	B
Private Timberlands	US Northwest (NCREIF)	7.59%	8.49%	C
Private Timberlands	50/50 South/NW (NCREIF)	7.14%	6.78%	D
Public Timber REITs	Forisk Timber REIT (FTR)*	6.65%	5.48%	
Equity Market	S&P 500	-0.48%	4.67%	

*Source: Forisk Timber REIT Index; share appreciation only

4. <u>Use weighted averages of NCREIF regional indices to match your portfolio and timeframe.</u> The table above includes four versions of the NCREIF Timberland Index over two timeframes, as well as the Forisk Timber REIT Index of public timber REITs and the S&P 500. Line "A" shows how the National Index returns vary by period. Lines "B" and "C" show annual returns for "South" and "Northwest" only timberlands, reporting how regional returns varied in level and direction. Line "D" includes a 50/50 weighting of the South and Northwest. The key message: **NCREIF can, and should, be matched to one's timberland investment portfolio as best as possible.**

SIDEBAR: What is a Timber Lease?

Generically, a lease is a contract in which the lessee (user) pays the lessor (owner) for use of an asset. With timber, the lessee grows and harvests trees on the lessor's land during the period of the lease.

Under a timber lease, the forestland owner usually receives equal annual payments, the amount of which gets negotiated up front. The lessee would harvest all merchantable timber from the land prior to the expiration of the lease.

Timber leases can vary in length, terms, and conditions. A forest owner in Louisiana called me about a 99-year lease associated with forests in his family. Instead of equal annual payments, the original lessor received a single lump-sum payment that equated to $25 per acre 75 years prior to our conversation. [If invested at 6%, that $25 would have grown to nearly $2,000.][13]

Why consider a lease for timberland? Landowners reduce risk through securing a continuous stream of annual income over the period of the lease. Also, the timber risk and management costs are transferred to the lessee.

Forest owners must pay attention to the tax implications. For more information on the tax treatment of leases, go to the "TimberTax" website on leases. Specifically, check the Internal Revenue Manual and the Specialized Industry Guidelines for Timber: Sub-Section 219.

---

[13] My thanks to Dr. Glen Melton for allowing me to share this example with you.

Risk, Risk Management, and Optionality in Forestry

Time is a distinguishing characteristic of investing in forests. Buying and planting tree seedlings for financial gain comes with an implied commitment. While the building you buy generates rental income next month, and the row crop you sow generates income within a year, the forest you plant returns cash periodically, with the first installment coming ten or more years in the future.

Once capital has been allocated, it is unavailable for other uses. That is about opportunity costs. So, we want a perspective on whether the decision to invest in forests meets our financial, operational, and portfolio objectives.

This section summarizes research and observations related to the risk, management of risk, liquidity, and optionality associated with timberland investments.

Real Options in Forestry

In graduate school, I conducted research on managing risk in forestry[14], which included the use of financial contracts, operational hedges, and "options" for timberland investors and forest owners.

Options? Yes, some view forest management as valuing and choosing between a series of real options. Research by leading forest investment professionals and economists Chris Zinkhan (1995), Andrew Plantinga (1998), and David Newman (2002) addressed versions of this theme, which focused on the traditional forest management problem of identifying the optimal forest rotation, and they applied real options theory.[15] Real option theory addresses limitations with net present value (NPV), which does not account for flexibility, volatility, and contingency with potential forestry investments.

---

[14] Mendell, B.C. (2004). *Managing financial risk in forestry and the forest products industry* [dissertation, University of Georgia].

[15] Zinkhan, F.C. 1995. The management of options and values. *Journal of Forestry.* January 1995: 25-29; Plantinga, A.J. 1998. The optimal timber rotation: an option value approach. *Forest Science* 44(2): 192-202; Newman, David H. 2002. Forestry's golden rule and the development of the optimal forest rotation literature, *Journal of Forest Economics* 8(1): 5-27.

What do flexibility, volatility, and contingency mean in the context of forestry? **Flexibility** refers to the manager's ability to defer, abandon, expand or reduce an investment due to new information or opportunities. **Volatility** references changing market conditions – particularly with timber prices – or new technologies that can alter the attractiveness of potential investments. **Contingency** refers to situations where future investments depend on investments made today. In theory, these options provide value and should be accounted for, or at least considered.

In practice, not all investors have the same levels of flexibility, exposure to volatility, or concerns about contingency. NPV analysis, which views decisions as fixed, is usually sufficient for making decisions. This makes real options analysis a whiteboard discussion for comparing and discussing a dynamic view of future choices for strategic planning.

Stand and forest level analysis centers on determining optimal silvicultural treatments and timber rotations, while accounting for product price risk and other uncertainties. Faustmann, through his work on BLV in 1849, established that forestry has perspectives on financial risk and opportunity cost.

At a certain level, forestry managers and timberland investors manage risk instinctively. This occurs through the normal calculus of assessing the risks and rewards associated with silvicultural treatments and timber sales, subject to financial risks emanating from outside of the forestry sector.

Pricing to Perfection

When acquiring and benchmarking timberland, a key risk is overpaying. This manifests in different forms. One is paying a premium price for an average asset or for an asset in a below average wood basket. Another way to overpay is to apply a valuation assuming perfect operational and biological performance of the forest and supply chain. How often do forest growth, harvesting activities, weather patterns, price forecasts, personnel decisions, and the economy mirror our expectations from a decade ago, much less last year?

When timberlands are "priced to perfection", they become harder to derisk and we worry about meeting financial goals and objectives. The localized nature of land and timber provide distinct investment opportunities. However, "pricing to perfection" can lead to the evaporation of localized differences if investors 'overpay' given the available information.

When evaluating a timberland investment property, apply multiple forecast scenarios and conduct a sensitivity analysis. In this way, you will be better prepared and positioned to manage risk and to value the property in a way that reflects a viable and operable outcome.

VIEW: When Might We Overvalue Timberlands?

In 1990, Nobel Prize-winning economist Daniel Kahneman and two colleagues published a study documenting how we can "overvalue" things we already own.[16] This "endowment effect" applies to investors who may retain assets beyond their strategic relevance, failing to account for true opportunity costs, and missing out on chances to reallocate that capital to investments that better suit their portfolios.

This issue reinforces the importance of making the best decisions given our understanding of current values and opportunities. That means, when considering investments, we look forward.

In forestry, we can struggle with "sunk costs." When testing the value of our timberlands against new investment opportunities, we must do so with ice in our veins and clear financial analysis. First, ignore sunk costs and, second, evaluate investments based on their ability to generate actual income and returns. The only time we have complete control over our portfolio is today.

When assessing our situation, revisit key questions, such as:

1. **Do my reasons (investment thesis) for holding the asset still apply?** If the investment diversifies my portfolio and generates cash as needed, then ignore the noise and focus on other issues. Your timberlands are doing what they were supposed to do.

2. **Have my timberlands reached financial maturity?** Have the costs of keeping an asset exceeded expected returns? Timber complicates this thinking because a tree is both the "product" and the "factory," which keeps appreciating over time by adding volume and value. Harvesting trees resets the production process. We check financial maturity by comparing the annual increase in forest value with the

---

[16] D. Kahneman, J. Knetsch and R. Thaler, "Experimental Tests of the Endowment Effect and the Coase Theorem," *The Journal of Political Economy*, December 1990.

investor's expected rate of return from other projects.[17] If we can do better elsewhere, we should feel compelled to do so. If we cannot, then grab a beer, sit on the porch, and enjoy the view.

3. **How do I evaluate short-term opportunities to enhance the performance of this forest asset?** Financial analysis often supports the "investment decision" by helping investors rank investment options and assess the impact of a given project on the forest. For example, marginal analysis helps quantify forest management and intermediate harvest decisions for existing stands. It answers questions of "when to harvest?" and "when does forest management pay?" and "should I accept this 'woods run' offer to harvest now?" Incremental differences in costs and benefits "on the margin" clarify decisions by focusing on the effects of a specific activity, not on the entire portfolio or investment.

Managing Risk as a Circular Flow of Funds

Forestry does not operate in a vacuum. Investors compare timberlands to alternative financial products, funds, and strategies. Capital flows around the world searching for the best returns relative to the associated risk.

Investors acquire timber with strategies that seek to maximize present value and returns. Anything that destroys assets, slows growth, or defers cash flows tends to diminish returns. Anything that increases present value faster than the investor's opportunity cost, often expressed in the discount rate, enhances value.

Managing the risk of forestry and timberland investments fits with the "circular flow of funds" approach to financial management, which focuses on two fiduciary objectives. One, raise and supply the funds required for timber-related investments on favorable terms. Two, use these funds effectively and efficiently to maximize returns. In short, raise money at low rates and invest it in trees at higher rates. Simple, right?

In practice, achieving these objectives depends on regular, consistent flows of cash to non-cash assets (forests and wood) back to

---

[17] My friend and timberland professional Robert Chambers observed, "The widely held belief that trees and timberland always add volume and value is not necessarily true…if timber prices decline at rates greater than the combination of timber growth plus grade ingrowth then value declines. This is true of trees and forests and does not consider the problems of estimating timber volume or value in-growth." Thank you, Bob!

cash. The cycle continues, assuming no disruptions in forest operations, local timber markets, acquisitions and divestitures, or administrative activities.

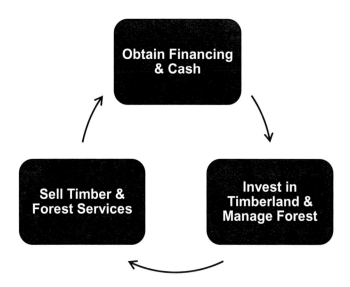

How do we measure timber investment success from this model? We look to make financial and operational decisions where:

- Cash flow circulates uninterrupted.
- Circle of cash grows and increases in value.
- Speed of cash flow accelerates.
- Circle continually spins off cash for other investments.

Thus, a benefit of the "circular flow of funds" approach is that it aligns with measuring timberland investment performance against specific, objectives. In short, it provides an effective way to keep score.

VIEW: Does Timberland Have a Liquidity "Problem"?

Liquidity – the ability to convert assets into cash – generally worries investors.[18] For timberland investors, the issue differs when buying shares in public timber REITs versus buying acres of timberland in Mississippi, just as buying shares of Ford Motor Company differs from

---

[18] Based on an excerpt from the Q2 2024 *Forisk Research Quarterly (FRQ)* feature article, "Topics on Forest Finance: Investment Criteria and Timberland Liquidity."

buying a Ford dealership. How can we frame liquidity in a way that provides context for timberland investors?

In my research, I find that the issue of liquidity varies by investor and over time, and that we are quick to generalize about the advantages and disadvantages of liquidity.

In finance, liquidity is a construct that affects certain folks in certain situations; it does not affect everyone always. Liquidity is a problem when you need it and don't have it. With timberland, liquidity comprises a set of issues that may relate or overlap. For example:

- **Leverage**: Debt differentiates during market crashes. While leverage has its role, timberland investors without debt cannot go broke or be compelled to liquidate during tough times with timber markets (though they may need to sell for non-timber obligations). Thus, liquidity is less relevant to the solvent firm. For highly leveraged organizations, debt compresses time and reduces options.

- **Valuations**: If we view liquidity as a balance of buyers and sellers at any given time, then in the absence of buyers or sellers, what is an asset worth? When traders scramble to pay debts and meet margin calls, they don't sell what they should, they sell what they can. Investors in comparable situations act surprised when markets tank and buyers are nowhere to be found. The best strategy: account for liquidity in advance.

- **Diversification**: Part of what makes timberland attractive includes return characteristics that rely on some "independence" from the overall market, which could, in part, reflect its illiquidity. The "indifference" of timberland to other assets helps make it diversifying. The frictions create an illiquid space from the high-volume flows for stocks and bonds. In practice, many assets are illiquid relative to cash, bonds, or equities. Cars and homes take weeks and months to buy or sell. While we can view this illiquidity as a constraint that limits short-term options, we can also see it as a protective moat that better preserves value (and wealth) for knowledgeable owners.

At times, timberland investors need cash. For example, due to irregular harvest revenues – a normal case for smaller timberland ownerships – the investor may need supplementary funds through a partial sale or from another source. The scale, time horizons, and opportunism required to manage timberland affects its liquidity. Partnerships, REITs, and secondary markets aim to mitigate this.

The liquidity implications for timberlands are asset and investor specific. Situations comprise a balance of time versus flexibility. While it helps to plan how you might unload a timber tract in a crisis, you get part-way there by breaking down the forest into its salable components, including timber, hunting rights, and choice parcels. Each sizable timberland asset comprises a diversified portfolio of smaller assets. The issue of liquidity for timberland is rarely all or nothing.

		Moderate Liquidity Low time pressure; limited options to generate cash other than divesting or borrowing against asset.	**High Liquidity** Low time pressure; multiple options to generate cash (e.g. increase short-term harvests, sell parcels).
Time Available	**High**		
	Low	**Low Liquidity** High time pressure; few options outside of selling asset or borrowing.	**Moderate Liquidity** Compelling time constraint; multiple options to generate cash.
		Low	High

Asset Flexibility

Consider situations where liquidity might matter. If you have an asset to sell, how long would it take, and would you net a satisfactory price (or return)? These questions get to the issue of time and flexibility. The inability to move an asset quickly may "cost" you something, and the need to accept a "below market" price because you are in a hurry may cost you something. In a crisis, illiquidity affects your ability to extract value, and in a market squeeze or crash, where sufficient buyers and sellers do not exist, you may be unable to move your asset at all.

In a presentation at the Federal Reserve Bank's 2005 Jackson Hole Economic Policy Symposium in Wyoming, economist Raghuram G. Rajan, then working with the IMF, noted how actual and perceived time pressure from excessive debt, unusual financial structures, or other obligations can essentially manifest losses through illiquidity. He observed[19]:

---

[19] "Has Financial Development Made the World Riskier?" 2005 NBER Working Paper available at: https://www.nber.org/system/files/working_papers/w11728/w11728.pdf

Liquidity allows holders of financial claims to be patient… and allows the value of the net financial claim to more fully reflect fundamental real value. Not only does illiquidity perpetuate the overhang of financial claims as well as uncertainty about their final resolution, a perception of too little aggregate liquidity in the system can trigger off additional demands for liquidity.

Overall, timberland investors are well capitalized and understand liquidity (and planned for it). They understand it's unlikely that many timberland owners will need to sell at a given time and over a similarly compressed timeline. If you have confidence that everyone holding the asset isn't going to run for the exit en masse, is illiquidity a problem?

Liquidity is largely a function of time horizon. Timber is a long-term play for long-term buyers and liquidity matters more for short-term sellers or investors reliant on significant leverage. In addition, investors may hold positions that are 'effectively' illiquid if they are too large or too small or too marginal in quality or location. When prices crash, it's easy to blame an absence of buyers on liquidity. From this view, liquidity is a problem for poor planners.

The relevance of liquidity to risk, returns, or cash flow varies across investors and over time. Liquidity thrives during periods of stability and of growth. Crashes, panics, recessions, and blackouts dry up liquidity. We only truly understand the value of liquidity when we don't have it.

Practical Considerations When Choosing Capital Projects

Economist Irving Fisher wrote: "**Capital value is income capitalized, and nothing else**." Capitalization refers to the conversion of expected income into an estimate of present value.

We consider all kinds of projects: reforest with better seedlings, build a mill, buy new skidders. What is the decision exercise? Specify criteria. Rank the projects against the criteria. Draw a line somewhere on the ranked list that says, "we would invest in the projects above the line, and those below the line scare us or conflict with our objectives."

Next, add up the dollars required for the good projects and figure out how to pay for them efficiently, if you can. Revisit the line. Discuss vigorously. This may cause you to move the line up (budget constraint) or move the line down (financing is cheap, hee haw!). When comparing the preferred projects to their budgets, dig in hard to confirm the ability of the organization to get them done well.

When reviewing projects internally or with clients, I spend time on the risks and worst-case scenarios. How do we mitigate them? Who will get this done? I've learned to think more and harder about the team involved. An okay project with a great team will outperform a great project handed to an unprepared crew. Just because the numbers look good does not mean the project fits the team. An attractive $1 million project handed to the wrong team produces a $1 million write-off...

Battle Scars and Communicating Results

During a field tour with forestry students in August 2005, Gary Brett, a forest business owner in north Florida, said, "I encourage you, do anything you can do to develop your communication skills, your people skills. It's about who can get things done, and that's about working with people."

Gary's message resonates with those of us who have dedicated careers and resources to working with forests, teams, and clients. Being effective and successful in forestry or finance requires skills beyond the technical. Success depends on our ability to communicate what we know to others. **This section summarizes best practices for minimizing analytic errors and maximizing our abilities to communicate the recommendations and results of our forest finance analysis to others**.

Investment Objectives Matter

While present value suitably ranks forestry investments for capital budgeting, other factors and objectives may influence decisions. Some forest owners prefer projects that maximize profits, near-term cash flows, or tax credits; others look to enhance wildlife habitat or recreational opportunities or forest carbon sequestration.

Herman Chapman, in his 1935 book *Forest Finance*, wrote:

Forestry is an empirical art and not a mathematical science. The two major premises upon which it rests, namely, human needs expressed in consumption of forest products, and the vital forces of tree life in their reaction to the composite factors of site including climate and soil, can be measured and predicted with only approximate accuracy. Yet upon these forecasts and appraisals the mathematics of Forest Finance must depend for its conclusions.

When making recommendations and delivering conclusions, it is our responsibility to be transparent and truthful in our assumptions and analysis, and practical and clear in communicating ideas. In the end, we do the best we can to account for the strengths and weaknesses of the data, as well as the objectives of the decision-makers.

What are Common Errors when Analyzing Forest Investments?

In analysis, **most errors relate to the data used – the inputs – or the math in the spreadsheet**. Errors with inputs affect the estimated cash flows, which impact value when discounted to today. We commonly find errors with assumed costs, estimated revenues, the timing of cash flows, and expectations associated with inflation and asset appreciation.

In our work and the work of others, we observe **three major categories of errors** in spreadsheet analysis and models.

1. Analytic errors. Across all the spreadsheet models we review, about one-third have an error in a formula (that we find). Often, these are associated with "relative" and "absolute" referencing, where a formula is pulling in data from the wrong cell or worksheet. Professor Ray Panko at the University of Hawaii, who conducts spreadsheet research (http://panko.shidler.hawaii.edu/ssr/), noted in a 2006 *Wall Street Journal* interview, that "you're going to have undetected errors in about 1% of all spreadsheet formulas."

2. Application errors. These refer to issues with the thinking behind the spreadsheet, the use of a formula, or a comparison made. Analysts can err by mixing real and nominal discount rates and cash flows, or by inappropriately comparing before and after-tax results and investments of differing duration (time periods). Also, using the incorrect metric can be problematic, such as misapplying cash-on-cash return, pay back analysis, or internal rate of return (IRR). We find errors of this type when analysts compare timberlands with bonds, manufacturing cap ex, and commercial real estate. Day-to-day metrics for forestry can differ, so spend time checking and thinking through the communication of results.

3. Errors of omission. These can be problematic and embarrassing. We work hard to avoid the situation of being asked "did you check _____?" and, if relevant, having to answer "No, we didn't think of that." Ugh. Unfortunately, analysis often omits key facts, relevant costs, and potential revenues. Confirm that assumed costs and revenues are current and reflect the best available, accessible information. Know what's knowable.

At Forisk, our team follows key practices to reduce the chance of errors. One, we **label tabs and worksheets, and date all files**. That way, when revisiting a model several weeks later, we can retrace our steps and thinking. Also, if we correct an error or make an improvement, we know which version is the most current.

Two, we **set aside time to check each other's work before sending results** "out the door." Admittedly, this is challenging. Setting and embracing milestones – midpoints for deliverables or reviewing work – throughout a project institutionalizes a level of quality control.

Finally, **we ask ourselves the question "where could we have blown this?"** Some level of paranoia and self-awareness is required for quality analysis of (forest) investments.

Prioritize Clean and Orderly Data and Analysis

Investors and managers often make decisions with imperfect information. Thus, we benefit by having an approach for dealing with uncertainty and minimizing errors when analyzing forestry investments.

When evaluating analysis, I start by confirming that what we have in hand is clean and accurate. Compiling a history of error-free, detail-oriented work builds trust and puts you in a better position to influence decisions and grow.

For strategy and market projections, I prefer clean data and analysis over rushed, subjective intel. Ideally, we have both. However, if given the choice, choose clean data and analysis, with an "as of" date, over speculation on today's unconfirmed prices or market intel.

Errors inject doubt. If a report has multiple errors, then I doubt everything it contains. However, if the analysis or research is clean but a little dated, we can still support decisions and assess performance.

Use Timelines Reduce Errors and Better Communicate Forest Investment Concepts

My graduate school advisor, Professor Mike Clutter, taught us to draw timelines when evaluating forestry investments. (On exams, he deducted points for failing to draw a timeline and gave partial credit if you did). Timelines reduce errors and communicate the timing of cash flows, the role of discounting, and the long commitment required of timberland investments.

To understand a forest investment and minimize a common analytic error, first draw a timeline to schedule the management activities and associated cash flows. Consider an example:

- Year 0: site prep and plant for $150 per acre
- Year 20: harvest 30 tons per acre at $25 per ton
  - 30 * 25 = $750 in gross revenue
- Discount rate: 6%
- Net present value (NPV) = $83.85 per acre

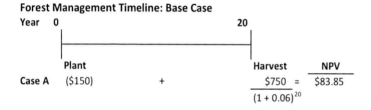

Forest Management Timeline: Base Case

Year 0 ──────────────── 20

	Plant		Harvest	NPV
Case A	($150)	+	$\dfrac{\$750}{(1+0.06)^{20}} =$	$83.85

Generally, site prep and planting occur, as on the timeline, at the beginning of year one, or "today", so the costs are not discounted. The harvest revenues occur at the end of year 20 and are discounted fully for 20 years. What if, however, site prep occurs later in the first year (beginning of year one)? What if harvesting occurs at the beginning of year 20 (end of year 19)? How can modest changes in cash flow timing affect NPV?

The following timeline plots four combinations for our example, with the NPVs based on simply moving cash flows for costs or revenues one year later or one year earlier. [Note: this example assumes the same harvest volumes. In practice, the volumes would likely differ by changing the time for forest growth.]

Forest Management Timeline

Year 0   1   19   20

	Plant	Plant		Harvest	Harvest	NPV
Case A	X				X	$83.85
Case B		X			X	$92.34
Case C	X			X		$97.88
Case D		X		X		$106.37

The results indicate the sensitivity of NPV from assigning cash flows incorrectly. We observe meaningful changes in NPV, even with cash flows off by just one year.

In short, **timelines help communicate forest investment concepts and strengthen results**. It is one thing to say "well, Mrs. Jones, we'll do site prep and plant trees in the first year, then fertilize and, at age 16, we'll thin the trees and then…" It is quite another thing to tell the story with a timeline and picture in hand.

Provide Context When Communicating Forest Investment and Sustainability Results

The growth of ESG investing – which screens investments and firms based on environmental, social, and governance criteria – and markets for forest carbon and other environmental "services" highlight the importance of clear communication skills. Timberland professionals regularly grapple with the most effective and "context appropriate" ways to answer question ranging from forest health metrics to rates of return.

Finance, investing, and forestry, come down to math. Consider reporting on forest sustainability versus investment performance. Financial returns often focus on percentages, which simplify comparisons. However, percentages communicate differently than dollar amounts. Saying "you earned 5% last year" differs from saying "you earned $5,000 on your $100,000 investment." They mean the same thing, but hearing dollar amounts clarifies the implications of how much wealth you gained.

The math of investments can, when reported as percentages, camouflage the dollar impact of fees, as well. Consider two descriptions of investment management fees:

"You will pay a 1% annual fee on this $1 million investment."

"You will pay a $10,000 annual fee on this $1 million."

The phrases describe identical fee structures differently. Do they sound or feel identical? The Securities and Exchange Commission (SEC) has, since 2004, accounted for this issue in shareholder reports and quarterly portfolio disclosures by requiring the reporting of fees in both percentage terms and in dollars per $1,000 invested.

The math of relative (percentage) measures versus absolute numbers applies to tree health and forest sustainability, which affects the reporting of forest carbon investments and wood bioenergy projects. Saying that a timber market "has a growth-to-drain ratio of 1.1", meaning growth exceeded removals by 10%, differs from saying "this market grows 1 million more tons than are harvested each year."

A percentage, while informative, provides incomplete information. We can always estimate performance in percentage terms, while absolute values, whether in dollars or tons or board feet, communicate the available cash, wood, or forestland.

What Opportunities Exist for 'Getting Smart' in Forest Finance?

I field versions of this question regularly from students seeking work in the timberland investment sector and from forestry professionals looking to broaden their skills and offerings to current clients.

Certain topics consistently generate questions from people who want to know about forestry and finance. These include forest owners, institutional investors, and other economic decision makers. In short, clients. The opportunity is to be and remain knowledgeable and strong in at least one of the following areas in addition to forestry.

1. Understand taxes. You can make or lose a lot of money based on what you know or don't know about timber taxes. Taxes matter. For example, tax laws encourage ownership changes. Issues associated with tax efficiency facilitated the movement of timberlands from C-corporations to institutional investors, real estate investment trusts (REITs) and subchapter S-corporations.
   a. Tax strategies that minimize capital gains taxes include the use of 1031 like-kind exchanges and installment notes.
   b. Capital gains and personal income tax rates differ. They affect optimal management strategies, net cash flows, and total forest investment returns.
   c. REIT tax rules differ from those applied to C-corporations, which affect equity returns and dividend payments.
2. Understand financial statements. They are the language of investors and executives. The results of managerial and capital allocation decisions get translated through audited financial statements that, like haikus and box scores, require interpretation and translation.
   a. While investors and analysts claim to like transparency, the reality is the reading and interpreting of financial statements requires practice and patience (and interest).

3. <u>Understand ownership structures</u>. Be able to explain a C-corporation versus a REIT versus other single-tax entities (LLC, S-corporation, MLP, etc.)
    a. Key implications include taxes, liquidity, costs, and ownership limitations (e.g. number of owners).
4. <u>Understand true risks (and accounting for them)</u>. Forestry novices ask about fire, bugs, disease, and hurricanes. Forest professionals can put these risks into context. Getting comfortable with timber risks means being familiar with physical, operational, financial, and regulatory risks. The long time horizons associated with forestry increase the need to understand the frequency and severity of key risks. Be prepared to answer, "how should we think about timberland risks?"
    a. Conversations of risk lead to discussions of appropriate discount rates. At a minimum, be aware of key benchmarks.
5. <u>Understand markets and forestry data</u>. Know current prices and industry trends. Timber prices provide a signal for the economics of a given wood basket today and historically. Prices consolidate all information known by participants in the market and summarize them in an easily shared form.
    a. Be familiar with indices and data sources such as the National Council for Real Estate Investment Fiduciaries (NCREIF), the Forisk Timber REIT Index (FTR Index), and the US Forest Service FIA database. Remember, all forestry data is a sample.
    b. Read industry magazines, websites such as Forisk's Blog, or newsletters published by regional forestry consultants.
    c. Remain aware of the health and status of markets for the forest products growing in your local market. Ask about changes to local wood-using mills, such as mill closures, expansions, extended downtime, and ownership changes.
6. <u>Understand how to communicate with a range of individuals</u>, in person and in writing. I wrote a book – *Loving Trees is Not Enough* – and speak on this topic because my mentors, starting with my parents, emphasized its importance. Forestry and investment analysts communicate with groups and individuals, including clients, executives, and colleagues. Our analysis has little value if it cannot be easily communicated. Be able to explain findings, assumptions, methods, and how they could help or affect others.

a. This includes the ability to show graphically, in clear and clean formats, the implications of quantitative analysis.

Finance Toolkit

One thing we can do to develop intuition and improve our financial analysis is simply increasing our comfort with math. Research indicates that focusing on math, rather than finance, leads to greater facility with money and investment decisions. **This chapter includes mathematical short cuts, investing strategies, and introductory tutorials intended to support the practical application of basic finance for evaluating investments and businesses.**

Finance Short Cut: Rule of 72

Want a **quick way to estimate the number of years required to double your money**? Divide 72 by the interest rate you expect to receive on your investment. For example, assume you have $100 earning 10%. Dividing 72 by 10 indicates it will take about 7.2 years to double our money to $200.

How accurate is the Rule of 72? We can use the Future Value formula to compare how close the Rule of 72 gets to the "actual" time for doubling our money.

$$\text{Future Value} = \text{Present Value} * (1 + \text{Interest Rate})^{\text{Years}}$$

Present Value	=	$100.00
Interest Rate	=	10%
Rule of 72 years	~	7.2
Actual Future Value	=	$198.62
Difference from $200	=	-0.7%

The Rule of 72 is within 1%. It supports quick math because 72 is easily divided by common rates such as 4, 6, 8 and 9. Our example shows that 7 and 10 are easily applied. Overall, the Rule provides a good estimate of investment growth <u>based on annual compounding</u>.

Use the "Rule of 69" for continuous compounding (though it's a bit curlier to divide quickly in your head). If doubling your money fails to warm your blood, consider the "Rule of 115" to estimate the years required to triple your investment.

Need inspiration? Billionaire investor Warren Buffett said, "My wealth has come from a combination of living in America, some lucky genes, and *compound interest*."

Dividend Discount Model

Want a **simple method for "valuing" stocks and income earning real estate or timberland**? Consider the Dividend Discount Model (DDM) by dividing next year's income, assuming it will be earned annually in perpetuity, by a constant discount rate or cost of equity.

$$\frac{\text{Price of}}{\text{Stock Today}} = \frac{\text{Dividend in Period 1}}{\text{Discount Rate}}$$

For example, assume Forisk stock pays $1.00 per share annually. How much would you pay per share if you require a return of 10%? According to the DDM, you would pay $10 per share ($1/10%).

Dividend	=	$1.00
Discount Rate	=	10%
Stock Price	=	$10.00

Apply this to forestry. Assume a timber tract generates $100 of net income per acre per year. Applying a 6% discount rate in the DDM ($100/6%) gives a value of $1,667 per acre. DDM gets us "in the ballpark" and provides a simple approach for "drive-by" valuations.

Note that the example assumes zero growth. A DDM version called the Gordon Growth Model, named for researcher Myron Gordon, accounts for constant growth of dividends.

$$\frac{\text{Price of}}{\text{Stock Today}} = \frac{\text{Dividend in Period 1}}{\text{Discount Rate - Growth}}$$

Using our previous example, assume that Forisk stock dividends grow 4% annually. According to the Gordon version of the Dividend Discount Model, you would pay $16.67 per share.

Dividend	=	$1.00
Discount Rate	=	10%
Growth Rate	=	4%
Stock Price	=	$16.67

Dollar-Cost Averaging and Investing in Timber

Regular and systematic investing, instead of trying to time the market, supports a commitment to building wealth. My Dad taught me about this by introducing me, years ago, to dollar-cost averaging.

With dollar-cost averaging, you regularly and systematically invest a fixed dollar amount, regardless the share or fund price. When prices are up, you will buy fewer shares, and when the market is down, your allocation pays for more shares. This strategy tends to result in a lower average cost per share over time when compared to lump-sum purchases. If in a retirement plan with monthly contributions, such as a 401(k), you effectively employ dollar-cost averaging.

In forestry, the easiest vehicles for a dollar-cost averaging strategy are the publicly traded timber REITs (PotlatchDeltic (PCH); Rayonier (RYN); and Weyerhaeuser (WY)). Investing in timberland is more complicated and costly on a per transaction basis. Dollar-cost averaging works best with low transaction costs and high liquidity. Public timber REITs have both.

The Forisk Timber REIT (FTR) Index is a market capitalization weighted index of the public timber REITs. Initiated in 2008, the FTR Index provides a useful benchmark for timberland vehicles and the overall market.

The table summarizes a dollar-cost averaging approach to investing in the timber REIT sector based on buying $10,000 of FTR Index "shares" at the end of each year for ten years, 2014 through 2023. With this strategy, the weighted average cost per "share" is $277.44, while the straight average of year-end prices was $285.21. As a result, your portfolio has more of the lower-priced shares and fewer of the most expensive shares, which lowers the weighted average cost.

Dollar-Cost Averaging with the Forisk Timber REIT (FTR) Index

Year End	FTR Price per "Share"	Amount Invested	"Shares" Purchased
2014	$270.52	$10,000	36.97
2015	$245.27	$10,000	40.77
2016	$257.64	$10,000	38.81
2017	$304.15	$10,000	32.88
2018	$199.05	$10,000	50.24
2019	$271.05	$10,000	36.89
2020	$304.01	$10,000	32.89
2021	$380.30	$10,000	26.29
2022	$293.80	$10,000	34.04
2023	$326.26	$10,000	30.65

Total Investment:	$	100,000
Total "Shares" Purchased:		360.44
Average Cost/Share:	$	277.44

The strategy is not always advantageous. If you had purchased $100,000 worth of shares at $270.52 in 2014, you would have been better off. However, this is hard to know in the moment. Therefore, think of dollar-cost averaging as a systematic way to cost-effectively invest over time.

TOOLKIT: Introduction to Financial Statements

Investment capital is finite in most industries, including forestry. Successful, profitable firms can accumulate capital for reallocation into new ventures and projects. Unsuccessful firms have their remaining assets liquidated for reallocation by others.

During these adventures, investors and executives balance three financial objectives: profits, financial condition, and cash flow. To do this, they monitor the economic performance of their businesses with three reports: the income statement, balance sheet, and statement of cash flows.

Here are summary observations about these tools, along with a highly simplified example of financials for the Faustmann Forestry Company.

Income Statement[20]

    The **income statement** provides a snapshot of financial performance. It is not cumulative, but captures revenues (sales) received and costs incurred for a fixed period, such as during a quarter or fiscal year. The intent of the income statement is to quantify earnings generated from core operations of the business.

    The income statement speaks to profitability. It is designed to be read and reviewed from top to bottom. Each line or section accounts for the numbers above until we get to the "bottom line" of net income (sometimes referred to as "net earnings").

Faustmann Forestry Company

Income Statement
(Thousands of dollars)

	2022	2021	2020
Net Sales	$ 10,400	7,600	6,800
Cost of sales	5,600	4,000	3,600
Gross profit	$ 4,800	3,600	3,200
Depreciation and amortization	$ 300	300	300
Depletion (cost of timber harvested)	$ 800	600	500
General and administrative expenses	1,300	1,200	1,100
Operating income	$ 2,400	1,500	1,300
Interest expense	$ 2,200	800	900
Income before income tax	$ 200	700	400
Income tax expense	$ 40	140	80
Net income	$ 160	560	320

    Watch gross profit (gross margins) over time. They offer clues. Deteriorating gross margins raises questions about operational performance and market assumptions or changes. Robust gross margins support healthy cash flows and earnings, and happy shareholders.

    In the case of Faustmann Forestry, we see gross margins, estimated by dividing gross profit by net sales, go from 47% in 2020 (3,200/6,800) to just over 47% in 2021 (3,600/7,600 = 47.4%) to 46% in

---

[20] My thanks to Shawn Fowler for helping me prepare this example. A retired partner from accounting firm Frazier & Deeter, Shawn and I once shared a room at a timber company board meeting, and stayed up late discussing forest finance and accounting. I use lessons and insights from that discussion to this day. Thank you, Shawn!

2022. Analytically, this does not raise major questions. Alternately, a situation with gross margins bouncing from 40% to 60% to 30% would require clarification and understanding.

Operating income, which nets operating expenses from operating revenues, offers a relatively clean way to assess business performance. It sets aside interest expenses and non-recurring items that have little to do with the day-to-day business model. Non-recurring items could include, for example, one-time write-downs or restructuring costs, or gains or losses from selling part of the business. Interest expense reflects financial policy and not operational performance.

On Faustmann Forestry's income statement, we see how operating income increased generally proportionally from 2020 to 2021 to 2022 with net sales, and this is consistent with the relatively stable gross margins over time. However, we also observe that interest expense nearly tripled from 2021 to 2022, from $800,000 to $2.2 million, so this raises questions with respect to debt and financing, that we can answer with the balance sheet and statement of cash flows.

When reviewing the income statement, keep in mind that cash, not net income, remains the most important measure of value and performance. A friend and former client of mine used to remind us that "cash is a fact; profit is an opinion." In other words, net income is an accounting number and may not reflect cash flow health.

Balance Sheet

The **balance sheet** measures cumulative performance. It also details the total investment (capital employed) in a business. By definition, the balance sheet *balances* total assets with total liabilities. They must always equate.

The balance sheet presents the current financial condition of the business. It does not report on cash flowing into or out of accounts; it simply reports ending balances. The income statement and balance sheet together inform shareholders about a firm's economic performance.

Capital structure refers to the types of capital employed to finance the firm's assets. This includes equity (common stock) and debt, which reflects a claim against future cash flows. Since interest is deductible, debt financing is viewed as cheaper. Increasing financial leverage can also increase the return on book equity. However, as debt levels increase, so do the risks of meeting fixed debt obligations. At some point, the risks outweigh the benefits as debt ratings fall and bankruptcy risk increases.

In the case of Faustmann Forestry, we see that long-term debt increased by $30 million, from $13 million in 2021 to $43 million in 2022, which helps explain the large increase in interest expense on the income statement over the same period. More debt usually translates into larger interest payments.

Balancing the increased debt is a $32 million increase in timber and timberlands in 2022. The larger timberland ownership helps explain the growth in net sales on the income statement, as harvesting likely occurred on more acres in 2022 than in 2021.

Faustmann Forestry Company	Balance Sheet		
	(Thousands of dollars)		
	2022	2021	2020
Asssets			
Current assets			
Cash and cash equivalents	$ 440	780	1,420
Inventories	2,800	2,200	1,900
Accounts receivable	800	1,000	900
Total current assets	$ 4,040	3,980	4,220
Timber and timberlands	$ 80,400	48,200	47,800
Property, plant, and equipment	2,600	2,900	3,200
Total assets	$ 87,040	55,080	55,220
Liabilities and Stockholders' Equity			
Current liabilities			
Accounts payable	$ 3,000	2,100	2,400
Deferred revenues	3,920	2,920	1,900
Total current liabilities	$ 6,920	$ 5,020	$ 4,300
Long-term debt	43,000	13,000	14,000
Total liabilities	$ 49,920	$ 18,020	$ 18,300
Stockholders' equity			
Common stock	$ 8,400	8,400	8,400
Retained earnings	28,720	28,660	28,500
Total liabilities and stockholders' equity	$ 87,040	55,080	55,200

On the balance sheet, net income accumulates in the retained earnings account. Retained earnings changes year-to-year by adding net income and subtracting stock dividends paid to shareholders, something we find on the cash flow statement.

A robust, healthy balance sheet provides management with financial flexibility, including the abilities to pay down debt, pay dividends, repurchase shares, invest in new projects, and, in the case of Faustmann Forestry, acquire timberlands. Unhealthy balance sheets constrain, handcuff, and limit opportunities.

Statement of Cash Flows

The **statement of cash flows**, also called the statement of changes in financial position, may be the most underappreciated financial statement. Taking time to understand it will provide a clear picture of how much cash the firm generated during the period and how the firm used that cash.

Faustmann Forestry Company	Statement of Cash Flows		
	(Thousands of dollars)		
	2022	2021	2020
Operating activities			
Net income	$ 160	560	320
Depreciation and amortization	300	300	300
Depletion	800	600	500
Changes in current assets/liabilities			
Accounts receivable	200	(100)	100
Accounts payable	900	(300)	(200)
Inventories	(600)	(300)	200
Net cash provided by operating activities	$ 1,760	$ 760	$ 1,220
Investing activities			
Capital expenditures requiring cash	$ -	-	-
Timberland acquisition	(32,000)	-	-
Net cash used for investing activities	$ (32,000)	-	-
Financing activities			
Proceeds from borrowing	$ 31,000	-	-
Repayments of notes payable and long-term debt	(1,000)	(1,000)	-
Stock dividends paid	(100)	(400)	(200)
Net cash provided/(required) by financing activities	$ 29,900	(1,400)	(200)
Net increase/(decrease) in cash	$ (340)	(640)	1,020
Cash and cash equivalents as of January 1	780	1,420	400
Cash and cash equivalents as of December 31	$ 440	780	1,420

The statement of cash flows tracks the sources of funds and uses of funds. Source of funds include cash from operations and cash from financing. Cash from operations is basically net income with all noncash items such as depreciation and depletion added back, along with changes in current assets and liabilities.

For example, in 2022, Faustmann Forestry generated net income of $160,000. To reconcile this with cash, we add back depreciation and depletion (both noncash items), and adjust for changes in accounts receivables, accounts payables and inventories (all tracked on the balance sheet). When accounts receivable decline, it means the firm received more cash (is owed less) than in the prior year. When inventories increase, the firm has less cash and, in the case of Faustmann Forestry, larger inventories of logs or real estate tracts or other items ready to sell that remain unsold.

Cash from financing can include, for example, borrowed funds. Faustmann Forestry borrowed $31 million in 2022, which closely aligns with the increased long-term debt on the balance sheet. Uses of funds include investments in the company and external distributions such as repurchases of stock, debt redemptions, and dividend payments to shareholders. In 2022, Faustmann Forestry invested $32 million in acquiring timberlands, which completes our understanding of why the firm borrowed funds and how those funds were invested.

Net cash flow equals cash generated from operations, less changes in working capital and capital expenditures. The statement of cash flows does not speak to profitability or the financial health (condition) of the business, as incoming cash from operating activities versus cash from financing (e.g. borrowing) differ.

Financial statements clarify the sources and uses of this cash, and how those uses (investments) are performing. Few things, if any, are more important for financial analysis than understanding cash flow. A firm's appeal depends on how much cash it generates from each dollar invested by shareholders or lenders.

Conclusion

Quarterly financial statements and annual company reports are the language of investors and executives, inside and outside of the forest industry. The results of managerial business and capital allocation decisions get translated through audited financial statements, which require interpretation and translation.

We use the Income Statement to ask questions related to profitability, sales targets, and expenses. We use the Balance Statement to evaluate the financial condition of the firm. We use the Statement of Cash Flows to analyze cash flow. Investments and firms function and survive on a continuous flow of cash. No cash flow, no business.

How to Read an Annual Report (if you only have 20 minutes)

Annual reports can yield valuable information, even if you are short on time. Reviewing annual reports can better prepare you for working with customers and suppliers. If you had 20 minutes, where should you focus? Think "L-L-C" to prioritize three things to better understand how a business makes money, how the leadership thinks (and who they are), and the performance of the firm.

1. **Letter**: read the Chairman/CEO letter. While some write this off as "fluff", it always includes business highlights (and lowlights, reasons, and excuses; make sure to know the difference). The letter will include noteworthy investments and efforts, and usually discusses the strategy and the business model.

2. **Leadership**: understand who runs the company, including the Board of Directors. Look at the makeup, backgrounds, and skills of those who control the company. Recent changes to the Board often highlight firm priorities.

3. **Cash**: confirm how cash is generated and used, including financing. Are the core operations generating cash? How is the company using that cash? How are they financing investments to grow the firm? The Statement of Cash Flows is straightforward once your eye knows where to go. At the end of the day, the numbers need to match the story.

If you have more time, read the Business Description to confirm the business model, business segments, key customers and exposures.

Recommended Resources

I use and recommend the following resources for better understanding questions and applications related to forestry and finance:

Corporate Finance and Valuation

- *Principles of Corporate Finance* by Brealey, R. and S. Myers 2001. McGraw-Hill Companies, Inc.
- Damodaran Online at http://pages.stern.nyu.edu/~adamodar/, the website of NYU finance professor Aswath Damodaran.
- *Valuation: Measuring and Managing the Value of Companies* by Koller, Goedhart and Wessels. 2010. Wiley.
- *Financial Markets and Corporate Strategy* by Grinblatt, M. and S. Titman. 2002. McGraw-Hill.
- *A Random Walk Down Wall Street* by Burton Malkiel. 2003. W.W. Norton and Company.

Forest Finance and Economics

- *Aunt Fanny Learns Forestry: Managing Timberland as an Investment* by B.C. Mendell. 2015. Forisk Press.
- *Basic Concepts in Forest Valuation and Investment Analysis* by Bullard, S.H. and T.J. Straka. 1998.
- *Timber Management: A Quantitative Approach* by Clutter, J.L., J.C. Fortson, L.V. Pienaar, G.H. Brister, and R. L. Bailey. 1983. John Wiley & Sons, N.Y.
- *Forest Management* by Davis, L., K. Johnson, P. Bettinger and T. Howard. 2001. McGraw-Hill.
- *Timberland Investments: A Portfolio Perspective* by Zinkhan, F.C., W.R. Sizemore, and G.H. Mason. 1992. Timber Press.

Timber Taxes:

- National Timber Tax Website at http://www.timbertax.org/
- Federal Income Tax on Timber by Haney, Siegel and Bishop. 2005. US Forest Service publication available at http://www.fs.fed.us/spf/coop/library/timbertax.pdf

Glossary

___

Bare land value (BLV): present net worth of bare forestland for timber production estimated over a perpetual series of rotations; also referred to as land expectation value (LEV) or soil expectation value (SEV).

Capital budgeting: process of identifying, comparing, and choosing projects or investments that generate the best financial returns or best meet investor objectives.

Cash flow: measure of investment or firm liquidity; comprised of net income plus non-cash expenditures (such as amortization, depletion and depreciation); notable saying: "cash is king."

Chip-n-saw: timber product from mid-sized trees used for dimension lumber and wood chips; name comes from the manufacturing process, which chips the outer slabs while the center cant is sawed into lumber.

Cost of capital: rate of interest a firm pays to secure financing (debt or equity) from investors buying the firm's stock or bonds.

Coverage ratio: measure for assessing how easily an investor can pay interest on outstanding debt; calculated by dividing net cash flow (or EBITDA) by interest expense.

Depletion: cost recovery method for natural resources; represents the costs we have in timber owned and harvested; subtract depletion from timber stumpage revenues to arrive at taxable income.

Discount rate: interest rate used to discount future cash flows; rate of return required to justify investment.

EBITDA: earnings before interest, taxes, depreciation, and amortization.

Equal annual equivalent (EAE): measure of annual profitability of an investment; annual payment that generates the estimated NPV of an investment. Helps compare investments with different time horizons.

Future value: value of an asset or investment at a specific future date.

Inflation: general increase in prices and wages over time and the associated (and unpleasant) reduction in the buying power of money.

Internal rate of return (IRR): discount rate that makes the NPV of a potential investment equal to zero.

Land expectation value (LEV): see "Bare land value."

Liquidity: indication of how easily (investment) assets can be converted into cash.

Maximum sustained yield (MSY): corresponds to a forest's maximum MAI; reflects the maximum volumes of timber that can be harvested sustainably without reducing a forest's inventory; age of MSY is also termed the "optimum biologic rotation."

Mean annual increment (MAI): average forest growth per acre per year over the life of the stand.

Modified internal rate of return (MIRR): version of IRR that assumes positive interim cash flows are reinvested at a specified rate; IRR assumes interim cash flows are reinvested at the IRR.

Net present value (NPV): present value of future revenues minus present value of future costs.

Opportunity cost: rate of return on the best alternative investment that is not chosen.

Payback period: time, usually stated in years, required to recover the initial investment in a project.

Pre-merchantable timber: also called "premerch"; refers to commercial species that are too young or small for sale to wood-using mills.

Present value: cash value today of future cash flows.

Pulpwood: smaller sized and lower quality trees used as raw material for fuel or paper production.

REIT: real estate investment trust.

Return on equity (ROE): net income, reported as a percent, on the equity invested into a firm, asset. or project.

Sawtimber: timber product from larger trees (larger than chip-n-saw) of good quality used to make lumber.

Soil expectation value (SEV): see "Bare land value."

Stumpage: value of standing trees "on the stump"; price of the trees that a landowner receives from a timber sale.

TIMO: timberland investment management organization.

Questions from Students

The following questions include those asked by students during and following participation in Forisk's "*Applied Forest Finance*" courses.

Q: "What is the difference between the cumulative returns and the average annual returns of an investment?"

A: The cumulative return is the total return of the investment over a specific period. This includes appreciation (capital gains) and reinvested distributions. The average annual return is the compounded annual return the investment would need to generate each year to produce the cumulative return.

If you invest $100 in timberlands for five years, it requires a 4.56% average annual return to produce a cumulative return of 25% ($125). Investors use these metrics to compare results across assets and benchmarks, such as the S&P 500, which are commonly stated in terms of annual returns.

Q: "What is a "basis point"?"

A: A basis point equals one one-hundredth (1/100) of 1%. In finance, one percent (1%) includes 100 basis points.

For example, a 0.5% increase in timberland returns would equal a 50 basis-point increase in returns. An increase in dividend yields for a share of stock from 3.75% to 4.00% is a 25 basis-point increase.

Q: "What is a 'yield curve'? I heard the expression 'inverted yield curve' on the news."

A: The "yield curve" shows the return (yield) offered by U.S. Treasuries of different maturities. Treasury yields refer to the total amount of money earned on U.S. Treasury bills (less than 1-year terms), notes (2 to 10-year terms) or bonds (longer than 10-year terms) sold by the U.S. Treasury Department to finance U.S. debt.

Treasury yields change daily because few investors hold them to term. Rather, they resell them on the open market. The slope of the yield curve changes over time and investors look to it as a signal or sign of economic health.

Typically, the government offers higher yields for longer maturities because investors require higher rates of return for locking up their capital for longer periods. The figure plots a yield curve based on U.S. Treasuries as of March 5, 2013.

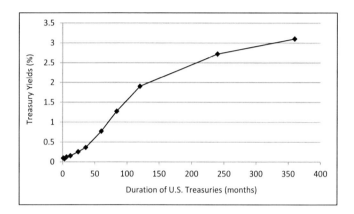

Analysts and economists often reference the yield curve when projecting the economy. What do they look for? A steep yield curve, where long-term yields exceed short-term yields, signals an economic expansion. When investors expect growth, they also anticipate higher inflation and interest rates, which may lead them to sell their long-term bonds. This drives down the price of bonds and boosts yields.

Alternately, an "inverted yield curve", where short-term yields temporarily exceed longer-term yields of bonds with the same credit quality, can signal an economic recession. Inverted Treasury yields occurred in April 2000, prior to the 2001 recession, and in January 2006, prior to the 2007 recession and in 2019, prior to the 2020 recession. Often, we observe temporary "partially" inverted yield curves. The table shows the yields from our figure above.

U.S. Treasury Yield Curve Rates as of March 5, 2013

Duration	1 Mo	3 Mo	6 Mo	1 Yr	2 Yr	3 Yr	5 Yr	7 Yr	10 Yr	20 Yr	30 Yr
Months	*1*	*3*	*6*	*12*	*24*	*36*	*60*	*84*	*120*	*240*	*360*
Yields (%)	0.09	0.08	0.12	0.15	0.25	0.36	0.77	1.27	1.9	2.72	3.1

Note that the yield on the one-month treasury exceeds (barely) that of the three-month treasury. Does this signal a recession? No. This inversion lasted one day, and investors quickly priced it out of the market. Rather, it can be viewed as a response to increasing long-term interest rates, which increased the demand for "short-term" credit. When demand for short-term borrowing goes up, banks can (temporarily) charge higher rates for this type of credit and borrowing.

Q: "What is 'forest rent'?"

A: Forest rent is the net earnings from forestland, including revenues and costs, estimated with the BLV formula using a zero discount rate. The public sector, at times, used forest rent to minimize the effect of compound interest and opportunity cost that drives down rotation lengths. From an economic standpoint, the strict application of forest rent minimizes the impact of the time value of money and leads to outsized, and underperforming, timberland investments.

Q: "Which is better for deflating prices in timberland valuation models, forecasts, and appraisals: CPI or PPI?"

A: CPI – the Consumer Price Index – highlights price changes (inflation) over time for consumers, while PPI – the Producer Price Index – tracks changes in selling prices received by domestic firms providing goods and services.

Typically, I use PPI for timberland and forest industry analysis because the growing and selling of timber or the manufacturing and selling of wood products represent, for the most part, business-to-business transactions. PPI better reflects the input costs into a manufacturing process ("producer" price index).

Q: "Is it fair to assume real prices increases of 1% or so over inflation in timber forecasts for valuation analysis?"

A: There must be a "story" to justify real price increases. Overall, timber prices converge regionally over time – up and down – to some range and, often, to a "pecking order" across wood baskets that account for timber quality and local markets.

Certain conditions can justify assumed real price increases for limited timeframes. These include returning to trend from events or economic cycles that pushed prices down; developing markets that have yet to mature; and verifiable supply or demand constraints.

Regardless, it is unreasonable, in my view and experience, to assume real price increases as a normal order of business or for long periods when modeling forest values. Doing so discounts the available evidence that timber prices decline in real terms over time, especially as wood using and timber growing technologies improve.

Q: "What is the appropriate timing of cash flows in a valuation model?"

A: In a forest operation, we often don't know if stands will be harvested at the beginning, middle, or end of a year. This can affect the results of DCF models and, for large ownerships, NPV estimates. If we assume all harvesting occurs at the beginning of the year, each cash flow will be discounted one year earlier, which leads to a higher NPV. If we assume all harvesting occurs at the end of the year, we discount all cash flows one additional year and systematically lower our NPV estimate.

In practice, we often assume harvesting occurs mid-year, at an "ownership" level across the property. Operationally, some timberland-owning firms incorporate the actual planting dates into their forward-looking harvest schedule models.

Q: "When estimating IRRs 'since inception' based on cash returns, why are timberland portfolios often zero or negative?"

A: Timberland investments often have periods of low or negative cash flows, especially when timber prices are low or harvesting activities are limited. Noting that a given tract of timber has negative cash flows for a given year tells us little about the quality of the investment. For example, replanted timberlands generate negative cash flows today and may ultimately represent robust, highly performing investments.

Calculating negative net IRRs that fail to include an assessment of current net asset value is like summing cash flows to date and subtracting the purchase price. This is "payback analysis" misapplied.

Q: "Can a BLV (bare land value) be negative?"

A: Yes. Friend and forest guru Chris McGarry reminded me of cases where BLVs can be negative. Sites with low forest productivity (low "site index") and high property taxes can generate negative cash flows over long time periods. This is especially true if stands lack supplementary cash flows from other activities. Slow growing hardwood stands in the North have cases that fit this profile and produce negative BLVs, too.

Q: "Does IRR provide a reasonable estimate for the risk-adjusted discount rate for a forestry investment?"

A: No. IRR does not provide a "proper" or "appropriate" signal for the risk associated with forestry or timber investments. Rather, it specifically, and by definition, provides the rate of return that produces an NPV of zero given the assumed cash flows.
        IRR does offer a good signal for the returns associated with our cash flow "story". Assuming we've accounted for concerns with the reinvestment rate (see "How and When do We Use IRR?"), IRR delivers a useful measure of investment performance in conjunction with NPV.

Q: "How do we account for the original timberland investment (capital) when evaluating new projects for the same forest?"

A: We don't. We evaluate new projects or investments "on the margin" and ignore sunk costs. We evaluate forest investments based on their ability to generate income and returns moving forward.
        Assume you paid $2,000 per acre for a pine plantation during a peak market. A new appraisal values this forest at $1,500 per acre, putting the investment under water compared to what you paid. Ugh.
        Then your forest manager calls asking for $100 per acre to fertilize the plantation. Her analysis indicates the fertilization will have an IRR of 20% over the next five years. Do we approve the forest manager's request and invest? Consider two perspectives.
        One, the fertilization is trying to "catch a falling knife" and throws good money after bad. Two, our forester's analysis of this investment on the margin looks attractive and we ignore the sunk costs.

We can't do anything about the $2,000 original investment. We completely control the $100 investment request. Does the fertilization create value and look like a good use of capital moving forward? Yes.

Q: "What financial techniques do timberland appraisers use?"

A: Appraisers apply three approaches to value timber properties: cost, sales comparison, and income. Timberland specific knowledge and experience is critical for the income approach, which requires estimates of future cash flows based on future forest growth and stumpage prices, and the use of discounted cash flow (DCF) models and analysis.

Q: "How can we value pre-merchantable forests?"

A: Pre-merchantable (premerch) forests have a couple of valuation issues. First, these stands have little ready salable volumes. Second, less comparable sales information exists for premerch timber. That said, premerch forest stands can still be valued with discounted cash flow models. While appraisals for timberlands sometimes apply a "cost" or "replacement" approach to premerch timber, it is still appropriate and doable to use DCF analysis.

I also recommend a 2007 article written by Professor Thomas Straka called "Valuation of Bare Forestland and Premerchantable Timber in Forestry Appraisal." He details the process for incorporating the value of the existing stand along with the BLV of future rotations.

Q: "What is the best economic metric or tool to rank or allocate capital for site preparation and planting? You know the situation – you have $XXXX dollars in the budget and YYYY acres to regenerate. The budget gets cut. How do we decide which acres get planted using strictly economic considerations (e.g. not include adjacency issues)?"

A: Assuming we have data on the relevant costs and productivity (e.g. site index, and growth and yields) for each stand, then bare land value (BLV) provides an ideal decision-making tool in this situation.

What makes BLV so useful for forest management? Relative to NPV and IRR, BLV captures all opportunity costs associated with the land. It also identifies the optimal economic rotation and strategy for each site. With BLV, we can decide whether, and where, to invest in specific silvicultural activities based on where they optimize value.

In practice, NPV and IRR are the norm for institutional investors, forest appraisers, and executives. Why? It's what they use every day for investment opportunities and projects outside of forestry.

Q: "Do we really need to manage forests to make money? Is it worth the extra effort instead of just letting trees grow on their own?"

A: In short, **yes and yes**.

Assume you own a 1,000-acre forest of pine in the U.S. South. Without intensive management, you could harvest 2,500 tons per year on a sustained basis. At $30 per ton, that produces $75,000 in annual cash flow. Your annual management expenses are $10,000, so you net $65,000. Assuming this cash flow in perpetuity with a 6% discount rate results in a net present value (NPV) of just under $1.1 million dollars ($65,000/0.06 = $1,083,333). That's $1,100 per acre.

With more intensive management, you increase the annual harvest to 4,000 tons. This volume reflects a higher performing forest growing more wood with shorter rotations. At $30 per ton, that's $120,000 in annual cash flow. You spend more, so your annual expenses are now $20,000 per year, netting $100,000. Assuming this cash flow in perpetuity at a 6% discount rate delivers an NPV of nearly $1.7 million dollars ($100,000/0.06 = $1,666,667). That's $1,700 per acre.

For timberland investments, active forest management charts the path to stronger cash flows and higher valuations.

Q: "Could you explain again why we grow larger trees?"

A: More volume and more value. In one of my first jobs at the log export yard in Cosmopolis, Washington, I learned that "12 is twice as much as 10." When scaling and sorting logs, a 12-inch diameter tree contains almost twice the volume of a 10-inch tree. Not only does the larger tree have more volume, but it also lets mills cut larger boards of greater value. For this reason, they pay more for larger logs.

In short, and of great importance to timberland investors, trees get more valuable as they grow into larger, more valuable logs for sawmills and plywood facilities.

Interview: *Mendell Looks to Local Factors for Timberland Valuations*

This excerpt is from the transcript of Curtis Seltzer's June 2010 interview with Brooks Mendell. Published by www.LandThink.com, it is reprinted here with permission and our thanks.

1. Do you think timberland is currently priced above, at or below market in terms of its intrinsic values (defined however you want), and why? What's driving current valuations? Do you see a change in valuation drivers in the future?

I worry less about regional or asset class-specific values and much more about individual properties and local timber markets. Timberland price-to-value metrics depend critically on the local wood basin and forest stocking level of the given property. Broad-based per-acre values used to evaluate regional averages can mislead investors into thinking they are performing at, above or below expectations. Over the years, key changes in valuation drivers include (1) the approach to building in HBU (development) opportunities into valuation models and (2) the selection and application of the discount rate. Today, rather than sifting through timberland properties seeking to find suitable development potential, investors are taking a forest-centric approach to evaluating timberland properties and asking, "what is this asset worth to me, assuming it will generate returns primarily from growing and selling trees?"

2. Do you use a general valuation formula for determining which investments to make, such as x% of acquisition cost in merchantable timber or a projected 10-year pay off of acquisition cost?

No. In supporting valuation work, we focus on two things. First, we clarify, possibly to the point of annoyance, the priorities of the investor. Being specific on this point is critical to any valuation efforts as it affects assumptions, investment periods and negotiations. For example, a client whose objective is to own forestlands from a "maximizing long-term returns" perspective differs from maximizing annual cash flows which differs from [owning] forests to help source a wood-using mill... to clients who prioritize recreational potential. We find, in cases, the clients themselves may not be clear on their own priorities, so we work through this to bring clarity to any valuation and due diligence work.

Second, we attempt to "know what's knowable" with respect to data for the DCF model, local wood markets, and client hurdle rates. We can review valuation models from a range of investors and analysts and find that, typically, ~30% have a math or Excel error, and most have made assumptions about costs, volumes or prices that could be strengthened with minimal work. So, in the DCF, we want, to the extent possible, "know what's knowable" and get it right relative to the investor's priorities. If we're not clear on what the investor values, the DCF can provide a valuation inconsistent with the true ownership objectives.

3. Do you anticipate any significant shifts in the market (positive or negative) for timber fiber/logs? Do you anticipate any [issues] that would positively or negatively affect markets for timber products?

The biggest downside risk for timberland owners may be unintended, negative impacts from legislation that narrowly defines wood-related raw materials that could qualify for bioenergy markets or subsidies, if there are any.

4. How would you advise small timberland investors to analyze an investment? How should they determine a buyer's price?

The recipe for analyzing timberland investments is straightforward, though it requires discipline and patience. First, understand the local wood market. Timber markets are uniquely local. The same timberland property in two different baskets will have two different values. Understanding the local basket goes beyond knowing all of the wood outlets into which you might sell trees. It includes knowing in advance how you will access these markets. Will you work through a forestry consultant? If so, who? Will you work directly with loggers? If so, who?

Second, question your data. In forestry, we have a somewhat bizarre relationship to data as compared to assets such as bonds, equities, or even commercial real estate. In forestry, everything is a sample. A forest cruise, which estimates the volume and value of the standing forest on a given property, is a sample of what's out there. If we use data from the US Forest Service, it's based on samples. If we use a timber pricing service, whether public or private, all reported prices are based on samples, not all transactions. So, ask questions about the data.

Third, and repeating a theme, know what's knowable. In evaluating the value to you, the investor, nail down, to the extent possible, what's left over each year after revenues are generated and bills paid. Be specific about what exactly will the property taxes be for THIS property, what are the annual management costs for THIS property, and what are the fees paid to consultants, accountants, and lawyers to acquire and manage THIS property. Plus, fully explore the revenue potential for the timberland property, above and beyond forestry. Cell towers? Mineral rights? Kaolin? Hunting? Spiritual retreats?

We recommend that investors become familiar with their local markets first, and then patiently seek and evaluate timberland opportunities. This approach leads to building solid models with tested assumptions for buying properties. Then, when the numbers look good, move fast.

5. Are there any game changers in the future that you've identified… for timberland?

We conduct a fair amount of in-house timber market and forest economics research to try and understand what makes timberland markets dance. Two areas continue to tickle our research funny bone. One, new seedlings could become forestry's "arms race." If clonal and related seedlings represent a leap in forest productivity, they could become a de facto requirement for competitive timberland returns. Two, ethanol and biodiesel subsidies could further drive up agriculture land prices, putting pressure on forestry-uses and timberland values. If you believe that ethanol markets are here to stay, and if you believe federal mandates – which currently dictate ethanol use – will continue to remain in place and may increase, and if you look at and believe the data linking ethanol production to food prices and supplies, then this is a plausible and supportable long-term investment thesis.

About the Author and Forisk Consulting

Dr. Brooks Mendell is President and CEO of Forisk, which he founded in 2004. His experience includes roles in forestry operations with Weyerhaeuser, in forest industry consulting with Accenture, and as a faculty member in forestry and finance at the University of Georgia. An award-winning speaker and writer, he has published articles and books on topics related to bioenergy, timber markets, timberland investments, forestry operations, business communications, and the MIT baseball team. A Fulbright Scholar and inductee in the Georgia Foresters Hall of Fame, Brooks earned B.S. and M.S. degrees at the Massachusetts Institute of Technology, an MBA at the University of California–Berkeley, and a Ph.D. in Forest Finance at the University of Georgia.

About Forisk Consulting (www.forisk.com)

Forisk is a research firm that delivers forecasts and analysis of timber markets and the forest industry. Forisk researchers have direct forest industry and analysis experience, including work in wood procurement, forest finance, forest operations, and economic forecasting.

Other Books by Brooks Mendell

- *Aunt Fanny Learns Forestry: Managing Timberland as an Investment* by Brooks Mendell, published by Forisk Press in 2015, 85 pages.
- *Wood for Bioenergy: Forests as a Resource for Biomass and Biofuels* by Brooks Mendell and Amanda Lang, published by the Forest History Society in 2012, 68 pages.
- *Loving Trees is Not Enough: Communication Skills for Natural Resource Professionals* by Brooks Mendell, published by Aventine Press in 2006, 112 pages.
- *Beaverball: A (Winning) Season with the MIT Baseball Team* by Brooks Mendell, published by Aventine Press in 2009, 200 pages.

Forisk Continuing Education Program

Forisk offers public and customized short courses and presentations on forest finance, timber market analysis, forest industry cap ex, and timberland investments. Forisk delivers these on site or virtually.